Ten Big

Communications

Disasters

By

David Ellis Heyman

Traveler's Lamp Inc.

© 2013

TEN BIG COMMUNICATIONS DISASTERS

Contents

Acknowledgements

In 1997, my father, Richard Heyman, wrote a great book called "Why Didn't You Say That In The First Place?" and it is the inspiration for this one. He's an internationally recognized communications expert and his book goes into great scholarly depth about the nature of human communication. I highly recommend it.

My mother, Phoebe Heyman, was a communications lecturer for many years, and inspired me to get my degree in communications. She gave me some excellent advice about this book.

My wife Sarah thought the book would be a good idea and supported my efforts at every step. She, too, gave me some excellent guidance on the book. I am forever grateful to her.

TEN BIG COMMUNICATIONS DISASTERS

About the author

David Heyman is a writer and communications consultant. He has a degree in communications from the University of Calgary and a diploma in broadcast journalism from the British Columbia Institute of Technology. After a 12-year career in electronic and print journalism in both British Columbia and Alberta, he became a communications advisor at various organizations, including the Office of the Premier of Alberta. He is now president of Traveler's Lamp Inc, which is focused on writing stories for print, TV and film.

He lives in Saanich, B.C. with his wife Sarah and sons Jonah, Sawyer and Henry.

Introduction

The following 10 chapters in this book are about people who failed to understand how human language works and, as a result, caused the deaths of others. They assumed people knew what they were talking about, when they didn't. If these people had just taken the time to be clearer with their messages, and made sure the people they were talking to understood, few if any of those involved would have died.

Misunderstandings between people are routine. Human language is not nearly as precise as we think. Each word we use depends on a mutual agreement on its meaning, based on the context of the conversation, not just its dictionary meaning. The words are the code and the context is the answer key.

For example, if you spent an afternoon with a friend watching an exciting regular season NFL game between the San Francisco 49ers and the Dallas Cowboys on TV, and at the end you turned to your friend and said "Some game!" he would assume you were talking about the game you both just watched. This assumption is so obvious that it's hardly worth mentioning, right? This is because you both share a context.

But notice you said just two words to your friend -- "some" and "game." Unknown to you, packed tightly into those words are dozens of understandings, recollections, images, feelings and thoughts about the great plays, controversial calls and funny moments. You unconsciously condensed all of that into a kind of "thought capsule" that you sent to your friend, who unpacked them in his mind a split second later and decoded them, using the context as the answer key.

Now imagine walking out of your house after the game and saying to the first person you meet "Some game." In all likelihood, he or she would have no idea what you were talking about. Your "thought capsule" would have failed because the listener didn't share a context with you. It could only have been decoded, with a shared context – watching the game together.

People who have been around each other for a long time – best friends, husbands and wives, or long-time employees of the same company – rarely make mistakes over context. Spouses will finish each other's sentences, and co-workers can just nod to each other to get their point across. They've shared so many experiences over the years they can predict the context of any conversation with great accuracy.

This system is not flawless, of course. Sometimes, even with shared contexts, we make mistakes by assuming a person means one thing when he or she actually means another. We were reading off the wrong answer key. Even best friends can make the wrong assumption but the fact is the less you know someone, the greater the chance to be misunderstood.

The following 10 chapters are about disasters caused solely by failures of human communication. In every case in this book, there were people who had enough information to prevent the disaster but who didn't make themselves clear to the people affected. They didn't communicate properly. They didn't mean for anyone to die but people did die because crucial information wasn't exchanged.

At the end of this book, there's a chapter called Code Red which explains how anyone in an important situation can communicate more effectively, to make sure they are understood. It's a simple method, but it works, whether you're hosting a party, planning a meeting or saving a life.

1

Tenerife

On March 27, 1977, Pan Am Flight 1736, a Boeing 747 jumbo jet, took off from Los Angeles International Airport with 366 people on board, on its way to the sun-soaked white-sand beaches of the Canary Islands off the northwest coast of Africa. The jet stopped at JFK airport in New York to pick up 14 more passengers and to change its crew before continuing onto the popular tourist destination.

The same day, KLM Flight 4805, another 747, took off from blustery, snowy Amsterdam's Schiphol Airport with 235 passengers, also headed to the Canary Islands with people looking to get away from winter.

As both planes were in the air, a small terrorist bomb was detonated in the main terminal at Las Palmas, the main city's airport, injuring several people, but fortunately killing no one. However, in order to do a proper investigation and to rule out the possibility of a second bomb, officials closed off part of the airport and temporarily diverted all incoming flights to a smaller regional airport at Los Rodeos, on the island of Tenerife, about 25 minutes away.

Tenerife was suddenly a very busy place. Within minutes, five airplanes from around the world, including the Pan Am and the KLM, began descending on the little airport, quickly clogging up the taxiways around the runway, jostling for space. The KLM passengers were allowed to disembark during the delay but the Pan Am passengers were obliged to stay.

A few hours later, officials at Las Palmas determined there were no more bombs and reopened the airport. Back at Tenerife, passengers were relieved to be able to reboard and continue their journey. One KLM passenger – tour guide Robina van Lanschot – had a boyfriend on Tenerife and chose to stay an extra day, a decision that saved her life.

But the planes could not continue their journeys right away. The KLM's pilot, Jacob Veldhuyzen van Zanten, had decided to take advantage of the delay by refueling, even though he didn't need extra for the short hop to Las Palmas. He knew there would be long lines at the main airport so he thought he'd fill up before he got there.

Unfortunately, his plane was still being refueled when Las Palmas opened, and while three other jets were able to take off from Tenerife, the Pan Am was stuck behind the KLM, unable to move until van Zanten was finished.

In the meantime, low cloud started to roll in off the Atlantic, which probably made both pilots tense up.

And to add a further problem, van Zanten was no doubt aware he and his crew were approaching their maximum allowable shift length according to Dutch law. If they didn't take off soon, they would be stuck on Tenerife, forced to take a mandatory sleep break, stranding their passengers overnight.

This delay probably irritated the silver-haired 50-year-old van Zanten. After all, he knew how important it was to be on time, for both pilots and passengers. And to force another plane full of people to wait while he

6

fueled up unnecessarily was probably an embarrassment to him. He probably would have thought such a faux pas for a pilot of his prestige would be unacceptable, something for which he might have chided his students.

After all, Van Zanten was literally the top pilot at one of Europe's premier airlines – he was KLM's chief flight instructor and, with 1,545 hours flying time on 747s, was in charge of training all of its 747 pilots. In fact, he was even the featured pilot in a two-page colour spread in the airline's on-board magazine that day. In it, he could be seen smiling under the headline: "KLM. From the people who made punctuality possible."

Ironically, it was van Zanten's desire for punctuality that day that may have doomed everyone on board his flight.

When the KLM was finished fueling, van Zanten was told to go eastward, to the end of the only runway, turn around 180 degrees, and then wait for permission to take off towards the west. The Pan Am flight was told to follow the KLM down the runway, but turn off left at the third exit, and then continue down the parallel taxiway to get behind the KLM flight for takeoff. They were told to report to the control tower when they were clear of the runway.

Both planes had to maneuver on the runway with low cloud hugging the tarmac, severely reducing visibility. Often, the fog was so thick the pilots could not see each other or the control tower. Making matters worse, the airport was not equipped with ground radar, as was standard at all large modern airports, so airplane crews were forced to rely exclusively on information from the control tower.

The Pan Am followed the KLM, with the American crew counting off the exits as they emerged from the fog. At first, the pilots were confused about which exit to take – did the control tower say the first one or the third one? -- and they called over the radio for clarification.

7

Air traffic control responded emphatically: "The third one, sir, one, two, three, third, third one."

But then they grew confused about which exit they should have started counting from – the first exit was clogged with planes so it was unusable. Did they mean to start at number 2?

When they reached what they thought was the third one, they were puzzled because it was at a 135-degree angle, meant for planes coming from the opposite direction.

The Pan Am crew then assumed the tower had miscounted, and were referring to the fourth exit, which had a much more manageable, 45-degree turn intended for the kind of maneuver they wanted to perform. The problem was, it was another 300 yards away, slow going, through the fog. They chose to drive to the fourth one, but didn't tell the tower.

At the same moment the Pan Am crew were rolling toward exit 4, the KLM jet had already turned around at the other end of the runway, and was waiting for permission to take off.

KLM 4805 – "The KLM four eight zero five is now ready for takeoff and we are waiting for our ATC (air traffic control) clearance."

Tower – "KLM eight seven zero five you are cleared to the Papa Beacon, climb to and maintain flight level nine zero, right turn after takeoff, proceed with heading four zero until intercepting the three two five radial from Las Palmas."

KLM 4805 – "Ah, roger sir, we are cleared to the Papa Beacon, flight level nine zero until intercepting the three two five. We are now at takeoff."

Tower – "O.K. Stand by for take off. I will call you.

Critically, the KLM crew heard only the "OK." The rest of the message was blocked by a simultaneous radio call from the Pan Am crew saying they

8

had not finished taxiing and were still on the runway. The two transmissions cancelled each other out with an electronic squeal.

The KLM crew advanced their throttles and their jet began hurtling down the runway through the fog directly at the obscured Pan Am jet which had yet to reach the exit.

Pan-Am 1736 – "And we're still taxiing down the runway (electronic squeal ends) Clipper one seven three six.

Tower – Ah – Papa Alpha one seven three six report the runway clear.

Pan Am 1736 – O.K., will report when we're clear.

Tower – Thank you.

The KLM crew, now accelerating rapidly, heard the tower ask the Pan Am crew to inform them when they had taken the exit and were off the runway. Startled, the KLM flight engineer wondered aloud if the Pan Am jet was still on the runway. But he was reassured by the captain the runway was clear and the KLM plane continued to accelerate.

KLM Flight Engineer (to KLM Captain) – Is hij er niet af dan? {Is he not clear then?}

KLM Captain – Wat zeg je? {What do you say?}

KLM Flight Engineer – Is hij er niet af, die Pan American? (Is he not clear that Pan American?)

KLM CAPTAIN – Jawel (An emphatic "Yes.")

Seconds later the crews see each other's planes about 700 metres away through the fog. The Pan Am crew initially think the KLM's lights are stationary but quickly realize their mistake. They steer their plan hard left, which was just about the only option available to them. Pan Am passengers were perplexed when they felt the giant airplane's front wheels leave the runway and roll onto the grass.

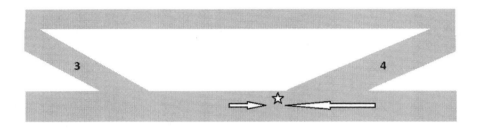

Diagram of the airport runway at Tenerife

Van Zanten now realized his terrible mistake. His 747 was hurtling at 180 miles an hour, and the 142,000 pounds of extra jet fuel he had just taken on would mean he would need more of the runway to get airborne than usual. He tried a premature take off and, with his tail scraping the runway; somehow he got his craft in the air, but not enough. While his nose and front landing gear cleared the Pan Am, the main landing gear and rear fuselage smashed into its right side.

The KLM landed another 150 yards away, and skidded another 300 while engulfed in flames, incinerating all 234 people aboard his jet. The fire was so hot it took 5,000 kilograms of foam, half a million liters of water and about 10 hours to extinguish.

The impact sheared the upper first class section off the Pan Am as well as nearly the entire top of the fuselage.

According to survivors, the shock of the impact was not excessively violent, and many thought the disaster was due to an explosion. A total of 56 stunned passengers and five crew members streamed out the emergency exits. Behind them were 326 passengers and nine crew, who perished in explosions, flames and smoke.

The crash still has the highest death toll from any aircraft disaster in history.

Investigation:

The official investigation into the crash was conducted by officials from Spain (which ruled the Canary Islands), the United States and the Netherlands, along with the two airlines involved.

The joint report of KLM and Pan Am Airlines was submitted on December 7th, 1978. It placed the blame for the accident squarely on the shoulders of van Zanten.

They concluded van Zanten made four critical mistakes:

1.   He took off without clearance.

2.   He did not obey the "stand by for take off" from the tower.

3.   He did not interrupt take off on learning that the Pan Am was still on the runway.

4.   In reply to the Flight Engineer's query as to whether the Pan Am had already left the runway, he replied emphatically in the affirmative.

The investigators knew many people would find it puzzling why someone with so much experience would make so many fundamental errors, so they also speculated on van Zanten's frame of mind at the time, and came up with some interesting insights.

Firstly, they felt there must have been some tension in the KLM cockpit due to the duty-time restrictions that were crowding their take-off window. According to Dutch law, the captain of an airplane is forbidden to exceed duty time, and can be prosecuted if he does. This wasn't always the case, and in fact Dutch law until a few years before the accident gave pilots some leeway, but as of 1997, the rules were very strict.

11

Calculating the time limit was also complicated, the investigators found. There were so many factors to consider that it couldn't be done in the cockpit, so the pilot has to contact the company to figure it out, as well as abide by its decision. In this case, van Zanten did contact KLM and was told he would have to take off soon.

"This uncertainty of the crew at not being able to determine their time limit exactly must have constituted an important psychological factor," the investigation found.

"Those who serviced the KLM plane in Tenerife stated that the crew appeared calm and friendly; nevertheless, they perhaps felt a certain subconscious – though exteriorly repressed – irritation caused by the fact that the service was turning out so badly, with the possible suspension of the Las Palmas-Amsterdam flight and the resulting alteration of each person's plans, which would be aggravated by the existence of other possible sources of lateness such as ATC delays, traffic congestion in Las Palmas, etc."

The weather was also a particular problem at this airport. It is at unusually high altitude for an island airport, at 2,073 feet, and it sits in a bowl surrounded by mountains that frequently has low-level clouds roll in from the ocean. These clouds can form and dissipate within a moment, creating uncertainty for take offs and landings. Again, this unpredictability would have been taking a toll on the KLM crew – a kind of emotional overload, the investigators said.

When van Zanten and his fellow crew members finally taxied to the end of the runway and turned around to take off, there must have been a feeling of exhilaration – a kind of let's-get-this-Boeing-going enthusiasm – that would have turned them partially deaf to any further need for delays.

The investigators also noticed something peculiar about van Zanten's own flight record. Although he had flown for many years, he had been an instructor for more than 10 of those years which would have reduced his familiarity with route flying. In fact, he had just spent six months training others, and the fatal flight was one of his first since rejoining the rotation. Investigators pointed out that when a junior pilot is in training, a senior pilot takes on the role of controller and issues take-off clearances. "In many cases, no communications whatsoever are used in simulated flights, and for this reason take off takes place without clearance," the investigators said.

There was also potentially a problem with hierarchy in the cockpit, though investigators admitted nothing abnormal could be deduced from the cockpit voice recording. "The fact exists that a co-pilot not very experienced with 747s was flying with one of the pilots of greatest prestige in the company who was, moreover, KLM's chief flying instructor and who had certified him fit to be a crew member for this type of plane. In case of doubt, these circumstances could have induced the co-pilot not to ask any questions, assuming that this captain was always right," the investigators wrote.

The co-pilot, First Officer Klass Meurs, had just 95 hours on 747s – and 9,200 total on any aircraft – that he probably didn't have the confidence necessary to overrule his much more experienced senior officer.

Flight engineer Willem Schreuder had more experience – 543 hours on 747s and 17,000 hours overall – and perhaps it was no coincidence that it was he who piped up at the very end to ask "Is he not clear then, that Pan American?"

Another problem identified by investigators is the focus of this book – unclear communication.

It was the KLM co-pilot, Klass Meurs, who told air traffic control "we are now at takeoff."

This is a perfect example of vague and ambiguous language at a critical time. It does not say exactly what is meant, and can mean two things to two different people.

Meurs meant his jet was taking off. The controller thought he meant he was waiting for clearance to take off. And since he had not been asked for take-off clearance, he wasn't going to grant it just yet.

The investigators recognized this faulty, confusing statement as a profound error, perhaps the most important of the entire day, and their recommendations reflected it:

In the future, they said, airlines and airports should place "great emphasis on the importance of exact compliance with instructions and clearances." They also said the industry should introduce "standard, concise and unequivocal aeronautical language" to prevent future misunderstandings. In particular, the industry should avoid the term "we're at take off" because of its ambiguity.

In the final analysis, the root of this crash was bad communication. There are many reasons for the bad communication – crew hierarchy, crew impatience, bad weather – but the simple fact is had the captain of the KLM spent a moment clarifying the position of the Pan Am before he took off, the crash would not have taken place.

As mentioned in this book's introduction, language is inherently vague and ambiguous. That is the normal setting for our interactions because otherwise we couldn't have time to exchange information and develop relationships because we'd always be clarifying what each other said.

We must all engage in assumptions about what is being said and why.

To their great credit, those who run the airline industry understood the problem and implemented exactly the right fixes.

In the 1970's experts discovered that human error – not faulty equipment or bad weather – was involved in more than 70 per cent of air crashes.

A NASA workshop examining the role of human error in air crashes found that the majority of crew errors consist of failures in leadership, team coordination, and decision-making.

Faced with this evidence, and spurred by the horrific death toll at Tenerife, the aviation industry made many changes to international airline regulations, top among them being the imposition of standard English phrases, and greater use of English as the common flight language.

In particular, the International Civil Aviation Authority addressed the specific problem with the term "take off" that caused the mayhem at Tenerife. Both pilots and air-traffic controllers are allowed to say "take off" only when the aircraft is cleared to speed down the runway and climb into the air. Before that, they should use only the word "departure."

Today here are many other standard phrases and terms of the ICAO, whose meanings are set out formally and all pilots must understand them:

To and For: These common English words sound just like the numbers "two" and "four," so pilots and air-traffic controllers should use "flight level" and "heading" immediately before saying any numbers. Such as: "US Air 565 climb to flight level 180" or "Lufthansa 119 turn right to heading 145."

Cleared: This word should only be used when talking about a clearance to take off or land.

Line up and wait – move into position but don't take off.

The ICAO also makes it clear that it's not enough to utter the right terms. You must also confirm the person you're speaking to understands you. And the best way to do that quickly is to have the listener repeat the phrase he or she just heard. In particular, any safety related message transmitted by voice must always be read back, it says.

These include instructions regarding:

- Taxiing

- Headings

- Speed

- Routes

- Approach clearances

- Runways in use

- Changes in radio frequency

The ICAO makes another important point – these terms do not and cannot cover every conceivable scenario. When in doubt, it says people should use concise and plain language to clear up any confusion.

Cockpit procedures have also been changed since Tenerife and other subsequent crashes and losses of life in the 1970s, when more than 70 per cent of air crashes were caused by human error, not equipment failures or the weather.

Hierarchical relations among crewmembers are played down. More emphasis is placed on decision-making by mutual agreement. This is known in the industry as Crew Resource Management, and is now standard training in all major airlines.

Crew Resource Management (CRM) is a series of protocols designed to make sure everyone involved in flying an aircraft – from the pilots and crew to the aircraft controllers – understands each other at all times.

CRM training manual for the Civil Aviation authority is specific on what people should and shouldn't do when flying an airplane.

It says when confronted with a problem, the crew should:

- Gather information and identify the problem.

- Review what caused it with other crew members

- Once a problem has been identified and diagnosed, the crew should:

- Say options out loud

- Ask other crew members for their opinions

- Review the risks and benefits of each option with the crew.

- Cooperate with each other by encouraging input and feedback.

- If you don't agree, talk and act respectfully to the others.

- If there is a conflict in the cockpit, keep calm.

- Concentrate on what is right, rather than who is right.

CRM recommends prior to every flight, the captain should hold a routine briefing with his flight and cabin crews. The captain should go over with everyone the intended course, flight plan, weather, potential delays and what he expects them to do.

A very important aspect of the CRM is that the captain doesn't just give a lecture, he asks his crew to repeat back to him what they heard – something called a "shared mental model." This verifies in the captain's mind that the crew has not only heard what he's said, they understand it, too. The crews also use checklists to make sure they go over all important items, even if they have the lists memorized.

17

CRM also breaks down hierarchies that naturally form in any culture between bosses and staff, senior employees and junior ones, men and women and the old and the young. These hierarchies may serve some kind of sociological purpose in society but they can be lethal in the cockpit if a junior officer is too intimidated by a senior officer to point out an error. The protocols focus on allowing anyone in the cockpit to raise a red flag, to point out errors, but also does it in a respectful way in order not to create any hurt feelings or being disrespectful, regardless of rank.

CRM deals with conflict resolution, by training crews to find ways to challenge the actions of others in a manner that doesn't cause discord. Co-pilots need to be able to raise safety concerns with their captains without worrying about being considered insubordinate. The saying is "find out what is right, not who is right."

Has this all worked? Absolutely, although it's impossible, of course, to say exactly how many crashes have been prevented. It's also difficult to say how much of an effect improved technology, design and mechanical procedures had in reducing crashes worldwide.

That said, the number of crashes of airplanes in the world that can carry more than six passengers – not including helicopters, balloons or fighter jets – has dropped steadily since Tenerife, according to the Geneva-based Aircaft Crashes Record Office.

According to ACRO data, 2011 was the safest year since 1977, with just 117 crashes, and 2010 and 2009 tied for the second best year with 133.

In fact, the top 12 safest years on record were all the years in the 2000s, almost in chronological order, as shown by the graph on the next page. (source: ACRO)

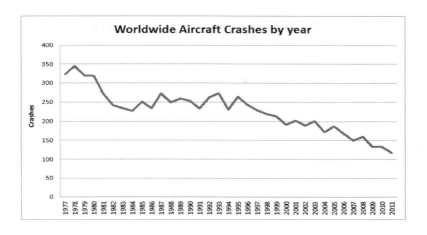

The number of airplane-crash deaths since 1977 is not quite so smooth a decline, though the trend is still very strongly downward. The eight years with the fewest deaths since 1977 have all occurred since 1999, and the fifth worst on record was 1977 itself. (Graph below: Source: ACRO)

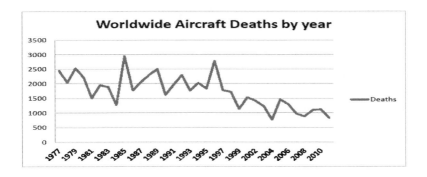

The aviation industry has not stopped with CRM. In 1998, a group called the Commercial Aviation Safety Team gave itself the goal of reducing the death rate in crashes in the U.S. by 80 per cent by 2008. By introducing CRM-style safety improvements, the fatality rate of commercial air travel in the U.S. was reduced by 83 per cent, CAST said. Its new goal is to drop the fatality risk a further 50 per cent between 2010 and 2025.

CRM has been so successful in the airline industry that CRM protocols have been adapted for use in the medical industry in the United States. Three authors from the Department of Psychology at the University of Texas at Austin wrote in 1999 that CRM-style training improved acute care by reducing medical errors. Some examples they cited were:

In Michigan, the infection rate in ICUs decreased by two-thirds with in the first three months of a widespread initiative to use checklists. The infection rates fell so low, they said, that the state's average ICU outperformed 99 per cent of ICUs nation-wide. They added the hospitals saved about $175 million and more than 1,500 lives.

A 19-item surgical safety checklist developed by the World Health Organization for eight hospitals around the world lowered the death rate within 30 days after surgery by 47 per cent. The checklist included many protocols that are now mandatory, such as:

• marking the body part to be amputated – something mandatory now in most countries.

• holding briefings, just like the ones in the cockpit, to ensure everyone in the operating room knew what their roles were

• checking that all needles, sponges and instruments were accounted for after surgery.

Furthermore, a study published online in 2006 by Health Services Research found the clinical error rate at a group of nine hospital emergency departments in the U.S. went from 31 percent to 4.4 percent in where CRM-inspired teamwork processes were implemented.

CRM training is now required for airlines in 185 countries by the International Civil Aviation Organization (ICAO), the regulatory component of the United Nations.

And CRM is also being used in industrial settings, including offshore oil operations and nuclear power plants. The training helps workers in control rooms and emergency command centers avoid making operational errors that may lead to accidents.

2

Halifax Explosion

It was the morning of December 6th, 1917 and the sun was just beginning to rise over Halifax, Nova Scotia when the captain of the French munitions ship the Mont Blanc ordered his crew to prepare to enter the city's harbor.

The ship had steamed from New York the day before with about 25,000 tons of explosives – mostly picric acid, but also some TNT, benzol and guncotton – but arrived late and was forced to wait overnight outside the harbor until crews opened the gates of the anti-submarine nets that had been strung across to keep German U-boats out.

In peacetime, a ship carrying such a dangerous load would be expected to fly a red flag to warn other ships of its cargo. The rule was relaxed when war began for fear of making such ships enemy targets.

By this date, the Great European Powers had been hurling massive armies of young men, bombs and steel at each other for more than three years. In that time, Halifax, with one of the largest natural harbors in the world, had become a vital link in the Atlantic supply chain that connected North

America to Britain but there was such demand to use the port it was often over crowded.

The approaching winter only made the situation worse, as Halifax was Canada's only major ice-free harbor. Ice had already taken hold in the upper St. Lawrence River, cutting off Canada's industrial heartland from direct sea access, so men and materiel had to be sent by trains to Halifax, to be loaded onto transports there. American, British and other allied and neutral vessels mixed with merchant ships to create massive traffic jams, with delays often lasting days

Therefore, when the authorities opened the gates in the anti-submarine nets every morning, there was an urgency to get through quickly in order not to have missions delayed further. There were many close calls and some collisions between ships headed by officers eager to get on their way.

The Captain of the Mont Blanc, Aime Le Medec, was not one of them. While his cargo was indeed important to the war effort, it was also volatile and he had no interest in rushing matters. On the other hand, he and his crew knew full well what was in their hold and it's hard to imagine them sleeping soundly while they were anchored overnight outside the protection of the harbor.

The anti-submarine nets also prevented ships in the harbor overnight from leaving and one of them was the Imo, a Norwegian-registered ship on a mission to bring relief supplies to Belgium, which at this time was occupied by the Germans.

The Germans were suffering through an Allied naval blockade and so they were seizing food and supplies for their armies that would otherwise have gone to civilians. Berlin, however, had agreed to let the Imo into Belgium as a humanitarian gesture and it was carrying a large sign on its side that said "Belgian Relief."

The Imo, empty on this morning, was scheduled to go to New York to pick up supplies before returning to Halifax to begin its journey across the ocean. It had been stuck in the harbor overnight because its coal shipment was late and by the time it was loaded up and ready to sail the nets were closed.

Its captain, Haakon From, was probably more eager than Le Medec to get on his journey. He and his crew had been confined to their ship during their stay to prevent possible mingling with German spies and may well have been eager to distribute their food and supplies in Europe.

At around 7:30 a.m. Canadian officials opened the gate in the nets and the Imo and Mont Blanc, along with many other ships, set sail. But before the Imo could get to open ocean, and before the Mont Blanc could dock, they both had to pass through a point in the main channel called The Narrows, a mile long and only about 600 yards wide.

There were strict rules for ships in the strait, but especially the Narrows, based on well-known rules of the sea. For one, ships had to pass each other on the right, just as vehicles on North American roads do today, to prevent collisions. In the event that a ship wanted to pass on the left, it had to give a short, single blast of its horn to its approaching counterpart. To confirm, that counterpart needed to respond with an equally short single blast of its own and then cross over to the other side.

If it didn't want to cross over, the second ship was obliged to sound two blasts, to indicate disagreement. In this case, the first ship would either change course or issue another single blast if it insisted on staying where it was.

If the horn blasts failed to sort out on which side the ships were to pass, they both were required to come to a full stop.

There was also a strict speed limit of five knots in the passage.

25

On its way out to sea this morning, the Imo encountered an inbound vessel, which witnesses said was an American "tramp steamer" and some historians identify as the SS Clara, though its true identity is not known for certain. This boat approached the Imo on the wrong side, the left side, contrary to the rules of the sea, possibly because it would make docking at the harbor easier for itself.

In any event, the Imo didn't object and switched over to its own left side, and the two ships passed each other without incident.

But the switch meant the Imo was approaching the Narrows on the wrong side. Making matters worse, it was speeding; records show it was moving at seven knots. Witnesses recall seeing "foam" on its bow from the churning sea water, a very unusual sight for such a busy port.

It was at this point the Imo and the Mont Blanc first sighted each other. The Imo issued a single horn blast indicating it wanted to stay on its left, rather than cross back over to its proper side on the right.

The captain of the Mont Blanc, whose ship was moving at a much-more-cautious four knots, signaled his disagreement with a double blast of his own. He also slowed his ship down even more and slid further to his right, edging precariously close to the shore. Because of his highly dangerous cargo, he felt any sudden move would be a bad idea, as it might shift his volatile cargo, causing a spark.

The response from the Imo's captain was yet another short single blast – he was insisting on staying on the left and demanded the Mont Blanc cross over, all the while maintaining his speed of seven knots.

The back-and-forth horn sounds drew the attention of hundreds of people on shore. They knew what the signals meant and, in anticipation of a collision, they stopped what they were doing to witness it.

At this point, the ships were just a few hundred feet apart and closing on each other fast. However, if they had simply maintained their bearings, they would probably have slipped by each other in a near miss as they weren't on a precise collision course.

Instead, both captains ordered evasive action and the result was catastrophic. The Mont Blanc moved hard to the left and the Imo threw its engines into full reverse. A moment later, at about 8:45 a.m., the bow of the Imo sliced a nine-foot gash into the right side of the Mont Blanc. After a few seconds, the Imo's engines, already in reverse, finally were able to yank the ship backwards but the friction of metal on metal as the bow was extricated sparked some of the picric acid on the Mont Blanc and within seconds the cargo began to smoke.

The Mont Blanc crew, knowing full well what was in their hull, rushed to their fire stations but the water hose system was damaged in the collision and they could not get enough water pressure. In any event, the captain deemed such an effort futile as he doubted spraying water on picric acid would have much of an effect. He ordered his crew to abandon ship, and while he intended to stay until the end, his crew eventually convinced him to join them in the lifeboats.

On the Imo, the crew were rather perplexed to see their counterparts madly scrambling to abandon ship so soon. The damage was above the water line and sinking wasn't a possibility for either vessel. Why weren't they staying to douse the flames? Or was there something in the cargo?

A rule of the sea at the time was that ships carrying munitions and/or explosives must fly a red flag. There was no such flag on the Mont Blanc, so the Imo crew ruled out that possibility. What they didn't know, what very few in Halifax knew, was the red-flag rule was optional during war time, in order not to alert enemy vessels of the cargo. Such knowledge would make any red-flagged ship an especially tempting target.

Within minutes, all the officers and crew of the Mont Blanc were off their ship and rowing madly to the north shore of the Narrows. Meanwhile, rescue crews from Halifax, including a fire boat, were rushing to the boat which was now drifting towards the Halifax shore. Like the Imo crew, rescuers were utterly unaware what was in the Mont Blanc hold.

The Mont Blanc crew, to their surprise, made it to the north shore. They had expected their cargo to detonate within a few minutes, maybe even seconds, but they were grateful to be wrong. They then began to try to alert the townsfolk of the impending disaster but the crew could only jabber away in the few words of English that they knew, while gesturing wildly. Their efforts at communication mostly just bewildered the people they encountered. Few understood and fewer still took precautions.

Meanwhile, the fire aboard the Mont Blanc was raging, spewing flames of wildly varying colours that entranced spectators and bewildered the military men, who could usually tell what was burning by the kind of smoke it made. The ship came to rest touching Pier 6 and set its wooden pilings afire, too.

The tugboat Stella Maris, which had seen the speeding Imo in the harbor blow by a moment earlier, was now on the scene spraying water on the blaze, to no effect. While two navy ships approached to investigate, the Stella Maris tried towing the Mont Blanc away, but it wouldn't budge.

On land, the Halifax Fire Department responded with 13 vehicles and crews tried to douse the flames from the shore.

Much of the population of Halifax and Dartmouth, the main city on the north shore, now watched the blaze with fascination. It was a cold day so most preferred to stay indoors and view the spectacle behind windows in their homes.

Making the sight even more interesting, the Mont Blanc cargo was being shaken by a series of explosions, sending even greater plumes of smoke into the air. Thousands of people, including hundreds of children, beheld the scene, often with delight, like an impromptu fireworks display.

And then, and 9:04:35 am...

The Mont Blanc vanished in a blinding, deafening explosion equal to the force of about three kilotons tons of TNT. It was the largest manmade explosion in history at the time. According to a 1918 report by Professor Howard Bronson of Dalhousie University in Halifax, buildings within a half-mile radius of the blast were totally destroyed. Even a mile away, structures were uninhabitable, and damage was even reported as far away as 10 miles. Some people in New Glasgow, 78 miles away, reported feeling the shock and a few said some items fell from their shelves. Remarkably, there were even a few people 225 miles away who said they felt or heard the blast.

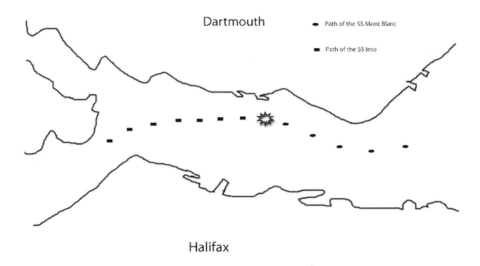

About 1,600 people were killed instantly; some blown into pieces so small their remains were never recovered. Headless and limbless bodies flew through the air. Dozens of people were hurled into trees and buildings where they lay dazed and injured. Hundreds more spectators, including dozens of curious children, suffered terrible eye injuries as window panes shattered in their faces. Many were permanently blinded.

A piece of the Mont Blanc's anchor landed more than two miles away while a gun barrel was thrown three miles away. The Imo was thrown across the harbor to the far bank, and most of its crew – including its captain and pilot – were killed.

The blast momentarily exposed the sea bed and caused a tsunami that washed up to 20 yards high.

But the misery of the survivors was only beginning. The shockwave had tipped over numerous wood stoves, furnaces and oil lamps, setting afire wooden houses and other buildings. Many of the injured died in the rubble because flames raged out of control. Even more would die in a bitter cold snap that followed the blast, as many had no way to heat their homes.

An entire Mi'kmaq aboriginal community of about 100 on the north shore vanished in the blast.

All told, about 2,000 people died and about 9,000 people were injured.

Exactly one week after the disaster, on December 13, 1917, Arthur Drysdale, a judge on the bench at the Supreme Court of Nova Scotia, opened a judicial inquiry into the disaster, officially called an "Investigation into the Mont Blanc and Imo Collision."

The hearing was held in a Halifax courthouse whose windows had been blown out by the blast and which had no power, but was structurally sound.

The inquiry ran to the end of January, 1918, hearing 61 witnesses over 19 days of testimony.

Drysdale focused much of his attention on what the Rules of the Road said about the disaster, in particular the concept that whichever ship sounded its horn first was the one that had priority.

The surviving Imo crew said their ship had blown its horn first, and the Mont Blanc had replied with a single horn blast to concur.

The Mont Blanc crew disagreed, saying their ship had sounded first, blowing just a single blast to warn the Imo it was going to stay to the right.

There were many neutral witnesses to the horns but they gave conflicting statements, some siding with the Mont Blanc and some with the Imo.

In any event, the Rules of the Road stated if there was a dispute, the ships were to come to a complete halt.

Judge Drysdale asked if there were any special rules for Halifax harbor and, to his surprise, was told no.

Fred Pasco, the acting superintendent of the Halifax dockyard, went further, saying there weren't even special rules for ships carrying explosives, not even one fully loaded and so obviously dangerous as the Mont Blanc. In fact, he said it had never even occurred to him "that a ship would be coming up a harbor like a piece of fireworks ready to be exploded."

He also said he was not aware of any narrow waterway in the world, aside from the Suez Canal, where one ship was required to stop to let another pass, as was the case in Halifax.

Collisions in Halifax harbor had happened several times in recent years, he said, but "I don't expect a ship to blow up because she has had a collision," he added. Pasco said he was also surprised shipping authorities would even allow a ship to carry such dangerous cargo, or that its crew would agree to man her.

Pasco's superior was Frederick Wyatt, the chief examining officer of the port who was in charge of monitoring harbor traffic, who agreed with Pasco that there were no special rules for handing ammunition ships.

He said he knew of the Mont Blanc and what it was carrying but on the fateful day he thought the Mont Blanc had the harbor all to herself. Since no ship had informed him of its intention to leave, and since all ships needed his permission to leave, he had assumed none was leaving port that day.

But on closer cross examination from a lawyer, Wyatt admitted this rule was not being strictly followed by the ships' pilots – local men who knew the harbor who were hired to steer the ships in and out. The departure of the ship was ultimately up to the pilot, not the Captain.

Wyatt admitted he had written a letter to his superior a few months prior to the disaster asking for permission to punish ship pilots who disobeyed this rule. He said the pilots often ignored the rules and set sail without notification.

His letter said, in part: "Under these conditions it is not possible to regulate the traffic in the harbor, and it is submitted that I cannot in this regard accept the responsibility of any accident occurring."

The inquiry later heard from some Halifax pilots, who said they knew about the rule, and were trying to obey it but often had a hard time reaching Wyatt. In some cases, they said, the pilots' clerk would deliver to his office long lists of vessels that had asked for permission to leave, but had long since departed, in some cases weeks ago.

James Creighton, the secretary of the Pilotage Commission, supported the pilots, saying his clerk, a boy of 15 years old, had given up reporting the movements of ships because he thought Wyatt didn't care anymore. The boy, who was also called to testify, said he had been making the daily reports but stopped because he thought the staff at the examiners' office was laughing at him and not writing the information down.

No pilot had been punished during this time.

Wyatt's credibility was further tarnished when a shipping official working for the Imo while it was in port claimed to have received a call from the examiner's office the night before the explosion asking if his ship had sailed. He told the person no, that it would leave the following morning. At best, that meant Wyatt should have known the Imo was leaving. At worst, he had lied on the stand when he claimed he thought the Mont Blanc had free passage in.

Wyatt was also asked what he could have done if he saw a ship leaving without his permission. He said he could have ordered it to stop by ordering the harbor's guns to fire at her. He said he had done such a thing but found not every order to stop was obeyed.

Wyatt's superior Edwin Martin took the stand and said he had not been aware pilots were having a hard time contacting the examiner's office, though he knew there were some general discipline problems. When shown the letters Wyatt sent, he said he didn't remember seeing them before but said he would have taken action if he had.

Drysdale's inquiry ultimately blamed Wyatt, Le Medec and the pilot of the Mont Blanc Francis Mackey for failing to follow navigational rules. Subsequently, they were all charged with manslaughter.

However, the charges against Le Medec and Mackey were subsequently dropped for being excessive, while Wyatt was found not guilty after the judge Benjamin Russell made it clear to the jury that Wyatt was too far removed from culpability to be found guilty of manslaughter, even if he had violated every rule in the book.

Later the owners of the ships sued each other for $2 million in a trial heard by Drysdale, the same man who had headed the inquiry, and he again found the Mont Blanc solely responsible.

The matter was appealed to the Supreme Court of Canada, which found the Imo and Mont Blanc equally at fault. The case then went to the British

33

Privy Council, which was at that time the final court of appeal in Canada, and it upheld the Supreme Court's ruling.

Wyatt was subsequently discharged from the navy for administrative, rather than punitive, reasons. They simply didn't want his services anymore – he had shown himself to be rather inept – and he didn't want to render them anymore.

The harbor also changed its rules so that only one ship at a time is allowed in the Narrows, a rule that still exists today.

Looking at the disaster today, if the pilots of the Imo and Mont Blanc had communicated better, their ships would not have collided. Primarily, they needed a quicker way to sort out who had the right of way.

The Imo's pilot felt he had it, due to the fact he had been pushed to the wrong side already by a previous vessel and would have had more difficulty making a correction than the oncoming Mont Blanc. The Mont Blanc, conversely, felt it needed to stay on course because of its volatile cargo. But none of this information could be communicated through the one horn-two horn system mandated by the international Rules of the Road. It was too simplistic and it broke down when it was required most. People should not expect a simple language, in this case the horn blasts, to be clear and useful in every case.

It should have been blindingly obvious to the captain of the Mont Blanc that he needed other ships to know how dangerous his cargo was. It seems that most everyone else in the harbor that day not only did not know what was on board, but didn't think such a cargo was possible, in the sense that no fool would ever load up a ship like that. Le Medec should have made sure the officials in Halifax knew what he was carrying.

So how could the ships have communicated better?

There needed to be a back-up mode of communication and the red flag was a good candidate for this. It would have told the pilot of the Imo immediately why the Mont Blanc was reluctant to cross over, and would have explained the consequences of further disagreement. The Mont Blanc's captain was understandably worried about flying the red flag at sea but he should have been flying it through the harbor. While there would have still been some worry about lurking U-boats in and around Halifax, once a ship was inside the area protected by the anti-submarine nets, the risk of being torpedoed would have been near zero, while the risk of collision with another ship – especially in the Narrows – would have grown. Therefore, it would have been better to have flown the red flag on the way into the harbor.

The two pilots could have contacted each other by radio, though there was no mention of the possibility in the judicial inquest, so the assumption in this book is such communication was not possible. Perhaps they didn't have radios on board, or if they did they couldn't be used to exchange messages on such short notice. Five years earlier, during the Titanic tragedy (discussed in an upcoming chapter), Morse code was used to call for help.

Ironically, electronic communication was used to save hundreds of lives after the collision but before the explosion. Train dispatcher Vincent Coleman was working with his boss William Lovett near a train station in the Halifax neighborhood of Richmond, just a few hundred feet from where the burning Mont Blanc came to rest.

Suddenly, a sailor burst into his office and told Coleman and Lovett the Mont Blanc was full of explosives. The two men started to leave but then Coleman suddenly realized there were at least two trains due at the Richmond station momentarily. Coleman sat back down at his telegraph set and tapped out Morse code warnings to stations up the line to stop their inbound trains:

"Hold up the train. Ammunition ship afire making for Pier 6 and will explode. Guess this will be my last message. Goodbye boys."

His warning was heeded immediately, and the closest train – with about 300 people aboard – was stopped just four miles away. More trains, some carrying passengers and others freight, halted at their stations further away. Seconds later, the entire neighborhood of Richmond was flattened, including the train station where Coleman sat. He died instantly.

Coleman's last message continued to benefit the residents of Halifax after the explosion. His warning was flashed throughout the entire Intercolonial Railway, so everyone knew immediately why the lines around Halifax went dead, and rescue operations began right away. Without such notice, help might have been delayed several crucial hours. By the end of the day, six different relief trains had pulled into Halifax.

One factor missing in the many analyses of this disaster is the speed of sound. Experts seemed not to have realized that when the ships first spotted each other, they were about three-quarters of a mile away from each other, or about 1320 yards. The speed of sound at sea level is 37 5 yards per second, meaning a horn blast from one ship would have taken a full three and a half seconds to reach the other. That is more than enough time to create confusion about whose ship blew its horn first. Even at half that distance, there was the distinct likelihood of misunderstanding whose horn sounded first. For this reason, it should also not be surprising that witnesses on the shores also had varying recollections about who sounded first.

To compensate for the delay, the captains and pilots would have had to wait several seconds to make sure the other ship had finished sounding its horn before starting its own message. This would have left less time to convey the important information before it was too late.

Could this have been the reason the two crews disputed whose horn was blown first? It seems more than possible. At the least, it exposes a serious flaw with the horn system of determining right of way in a tight channel.

The fact the Imo was speeding and the Mont Blanc was not flying a red flag makes them both at least partially culpable. If the Imo had slowed down, or the Mont Blanc had being flying a bright red flag, the accident might well have been avoided.

Ultimately, when dealing with life-threatening situations, lines of communication should be clear, and there should be back-up systems and redundancies if the primary ones fail.

3

RMS Titanic

The first warning of icebergs received by the RMS Titanic was about a day and a half before it actually hit one. It came via a wireless message broadcast by James Barr, the captain of the RMS Caronia, another British ocean liner, on the morning of April 14th, 1912, and it told of pieces of ice large and small in positions along the Titanic's route to New York.

"Captain, Titanic: Westbound steamers report bergs, growlers and field ice in 42 degrees north, from 49 degrees to 51 degrees west, April 12th. Compliments, Barr."

The message was taken down by the Titanic's wireless operator Jack Phillips, and handed to an officer who took it to the bridge, posted it on a wall and plotted the coordinates of the ice on a map. But the Titanic's captain, Edward Smith, took no action and his ship continued across the Atlantic at nearly top speed.

The weather for the Titanic's voyage so far had been calm and clear so Capt. Smith, on the urging of Bruce Ismay, the chairman and managing director of the ship's owner White Star Line, opened up the engines from the outset to test the ship's capabilities. On April 12th, the first full day at sea, the Titanic – the largest and most luxurious ship ever built to that point – covered 464 miles. On April 13th, it covered 519 miles, a speed of about 20 knots, delighting Smith and Ismay, who spent much of their evenings on board enjoying the elaborate parties.

A short time later, at 11:40 a.m., the Dutch liner Noordam told the Titanic about "much ice" in the same area reported by the Caronia. This message, too, was sent to the bridge. Smith again took no action. It was full steam ahead.

Twenty minutes later, by convention, the officers gathered at noon, grabbed their sextants, peered over the port side and calculated their ship's speed. The answer -- more than 22 knots, a blistering pace for any ship at that time and something for which White Star Line could be justifiably proud. Smith and Ismay agreed that on the 15th they would go even faster.

At 1:42 p.m. came a third message, this time from the RMS Baltic, that it had seen icebergs about 250 miles in front of the Titanic.

"Greek steamer Athenia reports passing icebergs and large quantities of field ice today in latitude 41° 51' N, longitude 49° 52' W. Wish you and Titanic all success. Commander."

Phillips ordered this message to be given straight to Capt. Smith, who read it and then gave it to Ismay when the two were having a late lunch.(Later in the afternoon, Ismay showed off the message to impress two ladies with whom he was dining, and put it back in his pocket.)

At 1:45 p.m., just moments after the Baltic's warning, came another one from the German liner Amerika, reporting it had just passed two large icebergs on the Titanic's route. Smith again took no action.

Sometime afterwards, in the middle of the afternoon, the ship's wireless went on the fritz. Phillips then dedicated himself to fixing it. But the primary concern of Phillips wasn't the icebergs, it was the dozens of civilian messages piling up on his desk. These were messages paid for by passengers wanting to use this wonderful new technology to boast to friends and loved ones back home of their voyage. The messages were usually of a trivial nature – "having a lovely time, weather pleasant" and such.

Although the content of the messages were trivial, their cost wasn't. Each message cost 12 shillings six pence for the first 10 words (between 50 and 400 pounds in today's money, depending on your method of calculation) and nine pence per word thereafter. In the 36 hours between Southampton and the iceberg, the ship's radio officers received and sent 250 passenger telegrams.

At 5:50 p.m., Smith figured the icebergs he kept hearing about were about to come in range, so he ordered his officers to steer a course about 10 miles southward, a very minor adjustment. In any event, he kept the ship at its speed and went for dinner.

At around 7 p.m., Phillips fixed the wireless and began working his way through the backlog of passenger messages.

At about 7:30 p.m. the Titanic overheard a message from the SS Californian to the Antillian about three large icebergs lurking just 50 miles ahead of the Titanic. However, for reasons unknown, this message was never posted on the board on the bridge or relayed to Capt. Smith.

At around 9 p.m. Smith himself arrived on the bridge for an update. The crew was alert for icebergs and expected to see them soon, but none had been spotted yet. After about a half hour, Smith told Charles Lightoller, the second mate, that he was retiring to his cabin for the night but ordered him to be alerted immediately if an iceberg was spotted. LIghtoller asked his night watch to scan the horizon for icebergs, but it was easier said than done. It was a moonless night, so the ice on the water wouldn't shine. Strangely, Lightoller refused the watchman's request for a pair of binoculars.

Capt. Smith's actions were also cavalier. He did not order his ship to change course any further, nor did he tell his officers to slow the ship down, even though it was now travelling at its fastest speed of the trip – more than 22 knots. It was a very clear night, but there was no moon so it was very dark. Worse, the calm seas meant it would be even harder to detect icebergs. In rough seas, the water splashes and churns around the edges of icebergs, and during the night the white "foam" can reflect what light there is quite well, putting them in a slightly starker relief against the blackness of the ocean.

At 9:30 p.m., the steamer Mesaba issued a warning of heavy pack ice and large icebergs. But this message, for reasons that are not clear, was not sent to the bridge. Had it been, and had the officers plotted the location of the dangers, they would have found themselves in the zone the Mesaba warned about.

At about 11:15 p.m., Phillips was still engaged in sending the backlog of passenger messages via a wireless station at Cape Race, Newfoundland, when the Titanic's crew saw mystery ship about 10-12 miles to the south, sitting still in the water. At about that time, Phillips received a wireless message:

"Say, old man, we are surrounded by ice and stopped."

The message not only startled Phillips but the volume nearly blasted his ears off because it was from a nearby ship.

Phillips snapped back: "Shut up! Shut up! I am busy working Cape Race!"

Phillips then apologized to the Cape Race operator and continued sending his passenger messages.

At around 11:39 p.m., one of the Titanic's lookouts, Frederick Fleet, spotted an iceberg, dead ahead, and he alerted the bridge, which reacted right away, calling for the ship to turn left and for the engines to be reversed "full speed" but it was too late.

For about 10 seconds, the right front side of the Titanic's hull scraped along a "blue" berg, an iceberg that had recently turned over and was still dark. There was now a series of dents, punctures and rips in the hull 100 yards long, through which ocean water was rushing. The first two rooms to be flooded were the mail room and squash court.

People on the ship sensed the collision in widely different ways. Some felt the ship rubbing against something, some felt a shudder, some felt a crunch and tearing, some felt a bump. Many felt nothing at all.

A few passengers went to the deck and saw thousands of shards of ice scattered everywhere. They were told by crew members not to worry, the ship struck some ice but everything was fine.

Captain Smith knew right away it was serious. He rushed to the bridge to find out what happened and was told the ship hit an iceberg. His first order was to close the "watertight doors" in the hull to contain the leak and second, for the engines to stop.

The Titanic's hull was divided into 16 compartments which were isolated from each other by bulkheads, except for small doors. It was those doors Smith wanted closed.

The doors were called watertight, but they weren't really, because the compartments were not closed at the top, meaning if one filled, it would spill over into the next one, which is what started to happen. The damage from the iceberg meant the front six of the 16 compartments were open to the sea.

As the engines stopped, an eerie calm took hold of the ship. Smith ordered a damage assessment but reports of flooding had already started coming in. The mail room was filling rapidly, said one.

When an officer asked Smith if that was serious, Smith said "it is more than serious" and asked that the ships "commutator" be brought to the bridge. Like a carpenter's bubble level, the device would tell Smith right away if the ship was listing one way or the other, before humans could sense it.

It was irrefutable – the Titanic was leaning five degrees to starboard and two degrees forward.

Smith and the architect of the Titanic, Thomas Andrews, went to Andrews's cabin to examine a scale model of the ship. There, Andrews showed Smith where the Titanic had been damaged. He estimated it would sink within two hours.

Both of them would have also known that there were only enough lifeboats for about half the 2,207 passengers and crew. The only hope for the other half was to be rescued which wasn't entirely out of the question. The Titanic was sitting in a major shipping lane and other ships were in the vicinity.

Simultaneously, on the Titanic, a lookout in the crow's nest spotted a ship to the south. The sighting was reported to the bridge. Through binoculars, the officers saw a vessel about a third the size of the Titanic, sitting motionless in the water on the southern horizon, about 10-12 miles away.

At 12:05 a.m., Smith was told about the ship to the south but did not immediately take action. He ordered the lifeboats uncovered and the passengers mustered on the boat deck wearing their life jackets. Officers and crew who had been asleep were awoken, and the news the ship had struck an iceberg spread to the passengers.

Smith then went right to the wireless room where he found Bride at the transmitter, having just relieved Phillips, who was getting undressed in a next door bunk to go to sleep. Smith told Bride the ship had struck an iceberg and to prepare to send an emergency message. Phillips overheard and began to get dressed again.

Smith left, got the position of his ship, and then handed the coordinates to Bride to send them out with an emergency message at once. Bride then gave the slip of paper to Phillips, who put on the headset.

At about this time, the Titanic's officers had learned about the ship on the horizon. Through binoculars they could tell from its lights it initially pointed west but had drifted to face the Titanic. They thought at first that meant it was heading towards their crippled ship but they soon realized it hadn't moved at all.

At 12:15 Phillips sent the message: "CQD MGY 41.46N 50.14 W"

CQ meant "all stations," D meant "distress," and MGY were the Titanic's call letters.

(CQD was still the conventional distress signal, even though SOS had just become the official standard.)

The distress messages were quickly acknowledged by several ships, many of whom then began racing towards the stricken ship. But the closest ship, the one on the southern horizon, stayed silent, and still.

At 12:25 a.m. Captain Smith ordered women and children into the lifeboats. At the same time, a ship called the RMS Carpathia responded that it was just 58 miles away and was steaming towards the Titanic at full speed, which meant she could be expected to arrive about 4 a.m. But the Carpathia's captain knew that wouldn't be quick enough, so he ordered extraordinary measures be taken to push her faster, such as shutting off heat to the passenger cabins so it could be channeled to the boilers. Although the ship's top design speed was 14 knots, the captain quickly had her doing 17, even through the ice fields ahead.

At 12:45 a.m., the first lifeboat hit the water, and the bridge ordered distress rockets be readied. Capt. Smith then focused on the mystery ship lying still in the water to the south. He ordered one officer to try contacting the ship with Morse lamp and then told another officer to fire the distress rockets which burst high above in the night sky, lighting up the ocean with a bang. Subsequent rockets were fired about every five-10 minutes afterwards.

Smith's officers told people in the lifeboats to row to that ship and return with the empty boats to take more survivors over.

At 1:15 a.m., the feeling on the bridge of the Titanic was desperate. Many ships were now steaming hard towards her but none had any chance of arriving before she was due to sink, with the exception of what was to them a mystery ship.

Now, with most of the lifeboats gone, their ship listing noticeably, and several rockets already having been fired in the air, the officers grew angry. Why didn't the ship on the horizon come to their rescue? A crew member had been trying for an hour to communicate with it via Morse lamp, to no avail. With no response, Phillips kept in communication with more distant ships, understanding the futility of their efforts. Phillips surely knew the ship was doomed, as long as that mystery ship stayed motionless.

At 1:40 a.m. the Titanic fired its eighth and last distress rocket

At around 2:05 a.m. the last lifeboat from the Titanic was dropped into the ocean. Capt. Smith then went to the wireless room where Phillips was still tapping out Morse code, and told him and Bride: "Men, you have done your full duty. You can do no more. Abandon your cabin. Now it's every man for himself." Both men ignored him and stayed where they were. Smith continued: "You look out for yourselves, I release you. That's the way of it at this kind of time," before leaving the wireless room. Phillips continued sending distress messages, but Bride gathered up some papers and the wireless log and left.

At 2:10 a.m., the Titanic's power was fading fast. Phillips sent out two letter "V"s before it went out completely, and that was the last anyone heard from the ship. The ship's stern was now pointing ever higher, and a series of crashes and bangs could be heard as chairs, plates and other pieces of furniture slid into each other and off shelves.

At 2:15 a.m., the bridge was submerged, taking Capt. Smith with it.

At 2:20 a.m., standing on a collapsible boat, fifty yards from the sinking ship, Second Officer Lightoller could hear shouts of hundreds of doomed passengers, adults and children, shouting "I love you" to each other as the Titanic disappeared from sight.

At 4 a.m. the S.S. Carpathia – which had responded to the Titanic's distress calls immediately and sailed selflessly at high speed through the ice field – arrived at the Titanic's last reported location. The Titanic was gone but, in the darkness, the Carpathia found a boat filled with survivors. At about this time, Phillips, the Titanic's wireless officer, died in another lifeboat. After having worked a 12-hour shift, then another two hours hammering out rescue pleas, he had jumped in the water at the very end and was scooped up by a leaking boat full of passengers. He had just enough energy to let his companions known several ships were steaming to the rescue. But the immersion in the 28F water sapped his remaining energy and he died. His body was slid back into the sea.

When dawn broke, the rest of the boats could be seen and rescue efforts began in full. And one of the ships that arrived was the S.S. Californian.

The day before the Titanic sank, the Californian, a freighter, was on its way to Boston when it came across three large icebergs. Its captain, Stanley Lord, ordered a warning be sent to the S.S. Antillian, which was also in the area.

"To Captain, Antillian: 6:30 p.m. apparent ship's time; latitude 42 degrees 3 minutes north, longitude 49 degrees 9 minutes degrees west. Three large bergs five miles to the southward of us. Regards, Lord."

The message was picked up by the Titanic and delivered to the ship's bridge.

Later that evening, the Californian suddenly encountered a huge ice field and Lord ordered evasive action. The ship came swung hard right, but not before bumping into several smaller pieces of ice.

With night falling, and not needing to be in Boston right away, Lord decided to stop for the night and wait until he had better light before proceeding through the ice field. But before he left the bridge to go lie down, he spotted the distant light of another ship apparently headed for the same hazard so he went down to the wireless room to find out if there were any ships approaching.

His wireless operator Cyril Evans said: "Only the Titanic." Lord then told him to tell the Titanic the Californian was surrounded by ice and stopped for the night.

At the same time, Lord's replacement on duty, third officer Charles Groves, also saw a ship on the northern horizon, and assumed it was the Titanic, due to its speed and its multiple, brightly lit decks.

Evans sent out the following message to the Titanic:

"Say, old man, we are surrounded by ice and stopped."

The message he got back was "Shut up! Shut up! I am busy working Cape Race!"

Evans shrugged. He listened to the Titanic's outbound messages for a few more minutes, and could tell his colleague was busy. He didn't feel like interrupting again, so he told his captain about the Titanic's response, and then shut off his wireless machine for the night. By 11:30 p.m. Evans was in bed with a book.

On the Californian's bridge, Groves told Capt. Lord about the ship on the horizon and that it was presumably the Titanic. Lord suggested trying to send it a message via Morse lamp, and Groves did so, but after a few attempts received no reply and gave up.

At about 12:45 a.m., Herbert Stone, the second officer, saw a flash of light above the Titanic and, a few minutes later, another, but he decided not to alert the captain right away. After the fifth, he changed his mind and went to see Lord.

"Are they company signals?" Lord asked, since rockets were a common way of communicating between ships, including those owned by the same company, for a variety of non-urgent reasons.

"I don't know, sir, but they appear to me to be all white," Stone replied.

Lord ordered Stone to continue the Morse flashing, and to let him know if there was an answer.

At 1:40 a.m. the crew of the Californian saw an eighth rocket fired. Stone and apprentice crewman James Gibson agreed there must be something wrong.

"A ship is not going to fire rockets at sea for nothing," said Stone.

But they continued to watch. Within a few minutes, Stone noticed the lights of the Titanic were changing and that one side appeared to be higher than the other.

"Look at her now, she looks very queer out of water," said Stone. "Her lights look queer."

They surmised the change was because the ship started to sail away, as its lights appeared to be receding into the distance.

But still more flares were sent up, and at 2:05 Gibson decided he needed to wake the captain up to tell him.

On the Californian, at 2:05 a.m. Gibson woke up Captain Lord and told him the ship had fired eight white rockets and then began steaming away. Lord asked if he was sure of the colour, and when Gibson said yes, Lord thanked him and went back to sleep.

By 2:40 a.m., Stone noticed the Titanic had disappeared, and sent a message to the captain about that fact. Again, Lord told him to record it in the log book, along with the fact the colour of the flares were white and went back to sleep.

At 4:00 a.m. chief officer George Stewart relieved Stone on the Bridge and got a rundown of the night's events. Stewart was startled by the news. The rockets were surely a cry for help, he thought. A few minutes later, Stewart woke Capt. Lord to make sure he knew about the rockets and he said he did.

At 5:30 a.m. Stewart woke up wireless operator Evans and told him about the flares and rockets. Evans was as shocked as Stewart. He quickly turned on his wireless unit and listened to the chatter from the other ships. His blood quickly ran cold. The Titanic had sunk.

Evans ran to Lord who immediately ordered his ship to head to the Titanic's last position. But by the time they got there, at around 7:30 a.m., there was almost nothing to be found, except for some floating wreckage and some overturned lifeboats. On the scene they encountered the Carpathia, which had already scooped up more than 700 survivors and was taking them to New York. The Californian spent a few hours more scouting the area but, finding no further survivors, left for Boston.

According to the British Board of Trade, the sinking of the Titanic caused the deaths of 1,514 people, with 710 surviving.

Only about one in five bodies was recovered.

In 1995, a joint French-American expedition located the wreck of the ship, 1,250 miles short of New York, and two-and-a-quarter miles below the surface of the water. Curiously, it was found 13 miles away from its wireless messages said it was.

There were two official investigations of the disaster – one American, led by Senator William Alden Smith of Michigan and one British, led by Lord Charles Bingham Mersey for the British Board of Trade.

In 1992, there was also a British reappraisal of the Titanic sinking, in light of the fact its wreckage had recently been found.

The U.S Inquiry found that the captain of the Titanic should have handled the messages his ship received with more organization. It ruled that if Smith had plotted the reported locations of ice, he would have found it was located on both sides of the lane his ship was in, and in the immediate vicinity of it.

And yet, the committee found, no discussion of the hazard took place among the officers and Smith called no conference to consider the warnings. He did not reduce the ship's speed, nor did he order more lookouts.

In his own conclusions, Senator Smith (no relation) said the Titanic failed to take even the simplest precautions against striking an iceberg, even though they were known to prowl that area of the Atlantic every year at that time. In particular, he said the officers should have at least given one of the lookouts aboard the ship a pair of binoculars.

"The Titanic rushed onward on her true course - one recognized as appropriate and agreed upon by mariners as the international highway for westbound vessels, yet dangerous at this season of the year, when the Labrador current may be bearing vast masses of ice across the track of ships," he wrote.

"Scores of these towering glaciers planted themselves in the very pathway of this ship, and were so large and so numerous that, in the absence of fog, they should have been easily discernible by the lookout, who says in his testimony that if he had been supplied with glasses, such as he had been accustomed to on the Oceanic, and on this vessel, between Belfast and Southampton, but which were denied him by Second Officer Lightoller between Southampton and the place of this accident, he could have seen the iceberg with which this ship collided, soon enough to get out of the way."

The committee also examined the actions of the Californian. After weighing the evidence, it found that the SS Californian was the only ship within range of the Titanic that could have arrived before it sank.

The committee looked at what the international rules were for signals at sea at night and it found these were the actions to be followed at night:

1.   A gun or other explosive fired every minute.

2.   Flames on the vessel, such as those from a barrel of burning tar or oil.

3.   Rockets or shells throwing stars of any color or description, fired one at a time at short intervals.

4.   The continuous sounding of a fog horn.

At the Senate inquiry, Capt. Lord testified his ship was about 19 miles from the Titanic, or far over the horizon, not the 10-12 miles calculated by the numerous officers and other witnesses on the doomed ship. He also said the meaning of the lights his crew saw was inconclusive. The committee found Lord hard to believe, especially since the pages from the Californian's log book that evening had mysteriously gone missing.

The committee ruled that the Captain and his crew failed to respond to obvious signals for help "in accordance with the dictates of humanity, international usage, and the requirements of law." And it criticized Lord for replying to the rockets with a mere lamp, flashed for two hours, rather than waking up his wireless operator to listen for any messages.

"In our opinion such conduct, whether arising from indifference or gross carelessness, is most reprehensible, and places upon the commander of the Californian a grave responsibility."

The committee concluded: "Had assistance been promptly proffered, or had wireless operator of the Californian remained a few minutes longer at his post on Sunday evening, that ship might have had the proud distinction of rescuing the lives of the passengers and crew of the Titanic."

Smith, in his own summary, was equally scathing of Lord:

"Had he been as vigilant in the movement of his vessel as he as he was active in displaying his own signal lamp, there is a very strong probability that every human life that was sacrificed through this disaster could have been saved."

As an example of what Lord could have done, Smith recounted the actions of Capt Arthur Rostron of the S.S. Carpathia, who immediately ordered his ship to the rescue on hearing the Titanic had struck an iceberg and was sinking. Rostron had been asleep at the time but his wireless operator was still awake, forwarding private messages from Cape Race. When the operator contacted the Titanic to pass on one of those messages, he was told of its predicament and alerted his captain right away. Rostron knew he had little chance of arriving on time, but he still pushed his ship to 17 and a half knots, a full three and a half faster than its rated maximum speed.

Sen. Smith said of Capt. Rostron:

"By his utter self-effacement and his own indifference to peril, by his promptness and his knightly sympathy, he rendered a great service to humanity... With most touching detail he promptly ordered the ship's officers to their stations, distributed the doctors into positions of greatest usefulness, prepared comforts for man and mother and babe; with foresight and tenderness he lifted them from their watery imprisonment and, when the rescue had been completed, summoned all of the rescued together and ordered the ship's bell tolled for the lost, and asked that prayers of thankfulness be offered by those who had been spared."

The British Wreck Commissioner's Inquiry began on May 2, 1912.

It said Capt. Smith could have done either of two things to avoid the ice that was in front of his ship: move significantly southward or slow down as night approached – but did neither.

But it did say Capt. Smith was justified in maintaining his course.

For at least a quarter century prior to the accident, when the weather was clear, ocean liners had been keeping to a customary track across the Atlantic that had been proven safe, since no lethal accidents on ships keeping to that route had been reported in all that time, even around ice. The disaster, however, proved the practice bad but only in retrospect.

"In these circumstances I am not able to blame Capt. Smith," said Lord Mersey. "He had not the experience which his own misfortune has afforded to those whom he has left behind, and he was doing only that which other skilled men would have done in the same position."

To the suggestion that Smith was being urged on to greater speeds by Ismay, Lord Mersey said the evidence disproves this.

"He made a mistake, a very grievous mistake, but one in which, in the face of the practice and of past experience, negligence cannot be said to have had any part."

But knowing that the sea lane was in fact dangerous, it would be negligent not to be more prudent in the future.

The inquiry also examined Capt. Lord's actions and it, too, summarily dismissed his suggestion he was too far away to have seen anything. And it also concluded Lord could have done so much more to save the Titanic's passengers.

"The night was clear and the sea was smooth. When she first saw the rockets the Californian could have pushed through the ice to the open water without any serious risk and so have come to the assistance of the Titanic. Had she done so she might have saved many if not all of the lives that were lost."

The Wreck Commission made 24 recommendations, including that all ships have enough space for everyone on lifeboats. But it is the 20th recommendation that seems the most obvious one today:

"That all such ships there should be an installation of wireless telegraphy, and that such installation should be worked with a sufficient number of trained operators to secure a continuous service by night and day. In this connection regard should be had to the resolutions of the International Conference on Wireless Telegraphy recently held under the presidency of Sir H. Babington Smith. That where practicable a silent chamber for "receiving" messages should form part of the installation."

In light of the fact the Titanic's wreckage had been found, another investigation was begun in 1988 by the Marine Accident Investigation Branch in Britain, headed by Deputy Chief Inspector James de Coverly, and completed in 1992

The investigator reappraised the evidence and concluded the Californian was actually between 17 and 20 miles from the Titanic – most likely 18 miles – which backed Captain Lord's testimony. But while the ships may not have actually seen each other, the Californian must have seen the Titanic's rockets, de Coverly found. Capt. Lord and his crew should have done much more than sit and watch the flares burst in the sky, he said, including setting sail towards them and turning on its wireless set.

The three official investigations into the disaster correctly homed in on the two great communications breakdowns that took place here – the failure of the Titanic's captain to handle the iceberg warnings properly, and the failure of the Californian's captain to be sufficiently curious about the rockets he saw.

Regarding the first failure, Capt. Smith actually had all the information he needed to avoid the iceberg that doomed his ship but he failed to organize it for the benefit of his officers. While it's perfectly normal for a captain to tour the ship and let subordinates steer, he should make sure they have all the information they need. In one instance, Capt. Smith actually wandered the decks carrying a note about an ice warning in his pocket for a few hours – information of no use to anyone outside of the bridge. Wireless technology was new, yes, but Capt. Smith should have seen its obvious potential.

The second failure was perhaps more egregious. Capt. Lord knew a ship nearby was trying to communicate, but failed to make even the most obvious attempts to investigate, such as waking up his wireless operator and turning on his ship's radio. It's even more bizarre that Capt. Lord's crew didn't think out loud, saying "maybe she's in trouble" or "perhaps we should move closer." There is some evidence Lord's crew was terrified of him and were afraid to bother him and that may have played some part.

In both major communications failures here, enough information was exchanged but it wasn't properly understood by the receiver. Capt. Smith paid for his mistake with his life and the lives of 1,500 others, while Capt. Lord paid for his with his reputation. Lord was never charged for his negligence he spent the rest of his life as a pariah. He died in 1962, never having expressed any kind of remorse for his lack of action 50 years before.

4

Victoria Hall

It was June 16, 1883, and all of the children in Sunderland, England were thrilled with anticipation. A well-known entertainer and his wife, Mr. and Mrs. Fay, were in town to perform at 3 p.m. at Victoria Hall, the town's main auditorium, with seating for 2,000.

To generate as much ticket revenue as possible, the Fays had gone to the schools around town the day before handing out tickets and handbills to "The Greatest Treat for Children Ever Given" with a performance that included "conjuring, talking waxworks, living marionettes, the Greatest Ghost Illusion, etc."

They gave teachers free admission if they distributed the tickets to their classes and all but one schoolmistress and two schoolmasters agreed to hand them out. The one-penny admission fee was to be paid at the door of the hall. But if any child was worried about the price, there was an enticement, printed near the bottom of the ticket: "Every child entering the room will stand a chance of receiving a handsome present, books, toys, etc."

Mr. Fay showed up at the hall around 12:30 p.m. with his sister, who was his manager, to set up and there was already a crowd of hundreds of kids. There to help Fay were just four men – Mr. Hesseltine, Fay's assistant; Mr. Wybert, Fay's general manager; the hall-keeper Frederick Graham, and Mr. Raine, an assistant to Graham.

Fay opened the hall to the public around 2:30 p.m. He tried to collect money at one entrance but found himself swarmed and so he set up at another place where the collection could be done in a more orderly manner.

When the show started, there were about 2,000 children in the hall – most of the town's population that was between ages 7-11. About 900 got good seats on the lower floor with most of the grownups but the rest had to go upstairs, where there were comparatively few adults, possibly as few as 20.

After many magic tricks and puppet shows, near the end of their show the Fays "hatched" some pigeons, which then flew around the room.

The time for the finale was at hand and it was time to hand out the toys and treats. Firstly, Fay asked Wybert to make sure all the doors were open and to ensure an orderly exit. Fay then gave a basket of gifts to Hesseltine with instructions to go up to the balcony and hand them out, so the kids there wouldn't feel left out.

Then Fay went back to the stage to perform his "hat trick" where he pulled several toys and treats from a hat and handed them to the children closest to him near the stage. He told the 1,100 children in the balcony they would get theirs as they filed out.

Fay himself noticed that while the children in the "pit" left in an orderly fashion, those in the gallery did not react to his announcement and appeared not to realize the entertainment was over.

The sight of some kids at the front getting gifts caused a frenzy among the children on the upper floor who then stampeded down a switch-back stairwell to make sure they didn't miss out.

The stairwell had 14 steps, each seven feet wide, in two separate flights. The second flight ended in a landing.

However, before the children could get to the stage for more gifts, they were impeded by a door bolted to the floor that intruded into the landing so that there was only a maximum 22-inch gap through which to pass – enough to let just one child at a time through.

The first few children slipped through but then two kids got wedged in the gap. Within seconds there was a crush of children behind them on the stairs pushing them from above. Quickly, the force of the surging crowd gave the children on the landing beside the door two choices – climb atop the pile or get fall underneath. Most fell and began to suffocate as even more children streamed from the stairs in the darkness.

Within seconds, the children had formed a pile several feet high and the screams of those on the bottom grew increasingly muffled.

Outside the stairwell, the adults remained unaware of the unfolding disaster. There were still hundreds of other children milling about, playing with their toys and streaming out of the hall on their way home. Fay was packing up his equipment.

The first adult to even partially appreciate the situation was Hesseltine, who was asked by Fay near the end of the show to get ready to distribute toys to the children in the gallery. Hesseltine was in the gallery during the "hat trick" and was handing out the gifts to children coming down the first flight of stairs when he noticed the crowd stopped moving.

"Pass along there," he said.

"We can't," shouted a child from around the corner.

59

Hesseltine then pushed his way through the crowd and out through the narrow opening of the door, which was now bolted to the floor. Then he noticed "an extra rush of children from behind him. He said he went outside to direct some children out another way, but came back to the bolted door and continued giving the remaining few gifts as children filed out through the door. Then he said there was another rush and the children were suddenly tangled together, and some started screaming.

It was at this moment that Wybert saw what was happening, and ran around to open a side door. Then Frederick Graham, the building's caretaker, also arrived after hearing some screaming and groaning from behind the door. He saw children piled up behind it, with Hesseltine trying to pull the door's bolt up. He tried to pull up the bolt on the door so it could swing open but the pressure from the other side had jammed it in, so he and Hesseltine ran outside and got into the staircase through another door.

At about four steps from the bottom, and covering the entire landing, Graham saw hundreds of children packed in a mass to a height of several feet.

Graham first tried to pull off children from the thickest of the mass but they were so tightly entwined from writhing and grappling to free themselves he stopped for fear he would break their bones. So he then switched to grabbing little ones from the top who were still showing signs of life.

Two more men showed up, and they began pealing injured children from the pile and handing them to a constable who took them outside to the open air.

By this time, the full scope of the horror was dawning on the adults in the town. Dozens of bleeding, crying and unconscious children were being rushed from the building. Still more were being carried out dead, and being lain in rows. Hundreds more were milling around, crying from the shock and looking for siblings.

Word quickly spread of the need for doctors, and parents who had been waiting at home for their children's return streamed down to the Hall to scan the crowd of survivors, or rows of the dead, for familiar faces.

Inside, the rescue effort was in full force. Hesseltine ran up to some stairs near to Fay and collapsed on his back, nearly fainting. Fay, who was oblivious, asked him what was wrong and Hesseltine couldn't speak. Fay ran to get some water for him but when he wouldn't drink it; he splashed it on his face. Hesseltine then spoke of perhaps a dozen or so children having died.

Fay then ran to the pit entrance and saw two or three other men running around, one with a boy in his arms, in front of some other boys lying on their backs.

"Are they dead," Fay asked, and a man said "Yes, there are a good many more dead. Run for a doctor."

Outside there were numerous heart-rending scenes. Some witnesses reported seeing a girl walking home with the body of her younger sister in her arms.

Other witnesses said one man and his wife, unable to find their children among the living outside, pushed their way into the hall to scan the dead bodies.

"That's one," he said, initially showing no emotion. Then he spotted a second child, then a third, and fell to the floor in grief.

""My God, All my family gone!" he said.

At least one family lost five children. A single Sunday school lost all 30 of its students.

In all, 183 children lost their lives – 114 boys and 69 girls. Most of them were between the ages of seven and 11 but some were as young as three. A further 100 or so were seriously injured.

On hearing about the disaster, Queen Victoria wrote a letter of condolence which was read out at some of the funeral services that followed. She said: "Suffer little children to come unto me, for of such is the Kingdom of God."

The Scottish poet, William McGonagall wrote a poem called "The Sunderland Calamity", to commemorate the terrible day.

A disaster fund raised about 5,000 pounds, which paid for the funerals of all the children, which took place over four days the following week.

Some money was left over and it went to pay for a memorial to the tragedy – a statue of a grieving mother cradling her dead child, which stands in Sunderland today, in a park across from the scene of the disaster, under a protective canopy.

Items from that terrible day are on display at a museum, including a wooden horse with its legs broken, thought to have been one of the prizes being given away on stage on the day.

As for Victoria Hall itself, it continued operating as an auditorium, minus the fateful door, for decades until it was destroyed by a German bomb during the Second World War.

Two inquests were called into the disaster because the victims were from a wide area – one for Bishopwearmouth, to be presided over by Mr. Crofton Maynard, and the other for Monkwearmouth, to be presided over by Mr. John Graham.

It was decided that the juries would meet together, have the evidence taken down in duplicate and then retire to consider their verdicts separately.

The inquiries focused much of their attention on who bolted the door to the floor. By all accounts the door was open before and during most of the show. But sometime just before the show ended, possibly just after, someone swung it out and slid the bolt into the floor, fixing it 22 inches ajar.

The prime suspect in this matter was Hesseltine, 22, whom Fay had given a box of toys to distribute in the gallery.

Hesseltine testified at the inquest, despite being warned by the coroner the inquiry could find him "culpably negligent." After the coroner told Hesseltine he could refuse to answer any questions if he wanted, he answered: "I will tell all I know."

Hesseltine said Fay told him to go to the gallery at the intermission to keep order, but stayed there until near the end of the show when he went to help Fay with the "hat trick." After that, Fay gave him the box of prizes to take back to the gallery to distribute and he said he stood at the top of the stairs and handed them out to the children exiting.

Hesseltine said he first noticed something was wrong when the crowd of children stopped filing past him.

"They seemed to stop in front and I shouted out 'Pass along there.' Someone said round the corner 'we can't,'" he told the inquest.

Hesseltine then said he pushed his way down the stairs and through the door, which he says was already bolted to the floor, and started giving out gifts from the other side of it, to encourage children to walk through.

Then, he said, there was another surge of children towards him.

Hesseltine: "I then put my box against the door and gave them what prizes I had, all but two or three small ones, and I said, 'You must all come out.' I pulled several of them out. Some were on their knees getting under one another's legs. After I got eight or nine out they seemed to be fast altogether. I could not move them any way. I put my hand round and I got out a little girl. She was the last one I did take out. I shouted for someone to come and see what was amiss at the door. One boy said, "For God's sake get me out! I'm fast (stuck)." Then Mr. Wybert came up to the door at the time. He came upstairs from the street entrance. He said, "I will go and open the dress circle door." And he went away again. Then a man like Graham came."

Coroner: "When did you bolt that door? Any amount of witnesses say they saw you."

Hesseltine: I did not bolt it. I put my hand down several times behind it, and I tried to take the children out."

Later, Hesseltine admitted trying to control the rush of children and admitted standing outside the door giving out gifts while the mass of children was on the other side of the door.

Coroner: "How do you explain these children telling us you were outside the door and that you put the bolt in?"

Hesseltine: "It is false, sir. I will swear it is false. I admit I was outside the door a long time, and I remember putting my hand down a lot of times to take the children away and pull them through."

Later:

Coroner: "What is your theory? How do you think the door got from the position in which it was when you went upstairs with the prizes to the position of being ajar?

Hesseltine: "I have not the least idea. I cannot account for it in any way."

The Coroner: "Did you attempt to get the bolt out?

Hesseltine: "I did not know there was a bolt there. At the time when there was not such a rush I could have got it out easily if I had known."

The inquest then heard testimony from several children who survived the tragedy, many of whom saw a man with a box of gifts put the door's bolt into the floor to control the crowd – a description that matched Hesseltine. However, they couldn't specifically identify Hesseltine as that man.

One such witness was nine-year-old Thomas Kent who was brought in from hospital with a broken arm to testify:

Coroner: "Was there a man about?

Thomas: "Yes. He was outside the door with a box."

Coroner: "What was he doing?"

Thomas: "He was coming up the stairs to give prizes away."

Coroner: "How did you know that?"

Thomas: "He was going to get within the door."

Coroner: "What prevented him?"

Thomas: "The children."

Coroner: "Did he do anything to the door?"

Thomas: "No."

Coroner: "Did he pull the door to?"

Thomas: "Yes. He pulled the door a little further than it was towards the outside."

Coroner: "Did you see him fasten the bolt?"

Thomas: "I saw him put his foot behind the door."

Coroner: "Did you see him do anything else?"

Thomas: "I saw him put the bolt in."

Coroner: "Did he say anything about the children?"

Thomas: "Yes. He saw a boy get five or six prizes, and said, 'This will never do.'

Coroner: "Did you try to get through the door to the inside?"

Thomas: "Yes."

A Juryman: "How far were you from the door when you saw him put his foot upon the bolt?"

Thomas: "Inside the door."

A juryman: "Are you quite sure that the man put his foot upon the bolt?"

Thomas: "Yes."

A juryman: "Was the man fair or dark?"

Thomas: "I don't know."

A juryman: "Did you see more than one man?"

Thomas: "No."

Coroner: "What was he trying to do?"

Thomas: "Shove the bolt in."

Coroner: "Might he not be trying to pull it out?"

Thomas: "No."

Coroner: What makes you think so?

Thomas: "Because it was out at first."

The inquest also investigated the question of who was responsible for looking after the children and for operating the hall generally. The coroner and jury spent a great deal of time trying to establish who was in charge of the building that day and to their surprise, no one took responsibility.

They called Fay himself to the stand and asked him if he thought having just four men to control a crowd of 2,000 children in a building he had never been in before was a good idea. He said he had booked similar halls all around Great Britain, and had entertained many more children at one time, with no fewer than four men for crowd control, and there was never any accident.

The town clerk, who was one of the jurors, also asked him why he distributed the gifts the way he did.

Town Clerk (an inquest juror): Did you not say something to the effect that the children should go quickly down to get them?

Fay: Oh, dear, no.

Town Clerk: Or that the first down would get the best prizes?

Fay: No.

Town Clerk: How long were you on the stage after you made the announcement?

Fay: I did not remain more than two minutes on the stage, and then I went into the body of the hall.

Town Clerk: Do you mean to say that there was no noise in the gallery immediately after you made the announcement?

Fay: No.

Town Clerk: Did the children not rush out?

Fay: They seemed to leave in the ordinary manner.

Town Clerk: Was there no sudden noise and rush to get out?

Fay: No.

Later, the coroner and other jurors asked him exactly what words he used to tell the children how to collect their presents.

Fay: I said the performance is now concluded, and I said that the children in the gallery would get some presents given to them as they passed out. Those are the words I used.

The Coroner: "The performance is now concluded," go on.

Fay: This concludes my performance. The children in the gallery will get some presents as they pass out.

Shield (another juror): That was an intimation to the children to leave the gallery, and leave it with the stimulus of getting a prize. At that time you did not know, did you, that there was any person in the gallery to see them come out?

Fay: I understood that the hall-keeper, Hesseltine, and Wybert were there.

Shield: You knew Mrs. Graham had been there half-an-hour before, but you did not know whether she had remained; you had seen Mr. Graham half-an-hour before, but you did not know what become of him in the interval?

Fay: No.

Newlands (another juror): You have had some experience in this business?

Fay: Yes.

Newlands: Has this distribution of prizes been followed by you for any length of time?

Fay: For about three or four years.

Later Fay was asked why he didn't have more adults to control such a large crowd of children:

Coroner: And you did not think it necessary to have oversight over these children in the gallery?

Fay: When I left the gallery I left the hall-keeper and his wife were there.

Coroner: Did you consider that sufficient adult attendance for 1,100 children?

Fay: I knew I had two men who would assist in getting them out.

Coroner: Did you not consider it necessary to have adult assistance during the performance? I never have anyone (helping me).

Another witness was Frederick Graham, the hall-keeper for the past 11 years. He said he first found out the hall had been rented at 10 a.m. on the Saturday, just five hours before the show was to start. He first met Fay at 2 p.m.

He said he told Fay not to use the dress circle (a middle tier of seats between the orchestra floor and the gallery) because it was the hall rule not to open it for under sixpence. He said Fay agreed, and then said he'd have to open the gallery.

Graham said he and Fay had problems controlling the crowd of eager children before the show started, just trying to collect their admission.

Graham: "When the doors were opened Mr. Fay was standing at a table along with myself. A crush of children came up, and Mr. Fay said it would not do, and he said something about his man being stupid to let them come up like that. He then left the table, went towards the door where the accident took place, and I thought he was going to check the children. I cannot say how far he was. He was away about half a minute."

Coroner: "Could he get to the door in that time?"

Graham: "Yes. The children still came on, and there was such a crush that the children commenced to move about, and he said he could not take the money there, but would go to the top of the gallery stairs and do it. When he went up to the top of the stairs I shifted the table into the corner, and I went up to the gallery to find Mr. Fay. I was keeping the children back, and Mr. Fay took the money. I continued doing that till near three o'clock, when Mr. Fay went away from the gallery. I took some coppers after Mr. Fay went away."

Graham estimated there were only two or three adults in the gallery prior to the show.

Coroner: "After Mr. Fay went away who was left in charge of the gallery?"

Graham: "My wife was there."

Coroner: "Did you consider yourself in charge there?"

Graham: "No."

Coroner: "Then why were you there?"

Graham: "Simply to assist on account of the pressure of children."

The coroner and jury then wondered if neither the hall-keeper nor the renter was in charge of the crowd, who was? They were also troubled by the fact Graham said he didn't even consider it his job to familiarize the renters of the hall with the building, including showing them that the fateful door could be bolted to the floor.

Coroner: When strangers come you leave them to go down and open the doors themselves?

Graham: That is the usual way.

Mr. Shield: Do you not give strangers instructions about the hall?

Graham: "Without ever saying a word or asking a question they sometimes rush off and make their arrangements immediately."

Shield: "Do you consider the building a building of complication?

Graham: "Well, yes."

Shield: "Do you not consider it reasonable that you should show people all over the hall?

Graham: "I cannot say, sir."

A Juryman: "You will have to do it in the future."

Shield: "Did you ever say that the door could be bolted back?

Graham: "No."

Shield: "You do not suggest to strangers that the door should be bolted back?"

Graham: "No."

Subsequent witnesses to the inquiry were Frederick Taylor, the sole proprietor of the hall, who was in charge of renting it out. He said unequivocally that he considered renters responsible for the use of the hall. As for the door, Taylor said it never caused a problem in the past but only became a problem "through a combination of peculiar circumstances." However, he did say the door should be altered to make it safer, but not removed.

Another witness was a Mr. Coates, the managing clerk for the building's owner, a Mr. T.L. Howarth. Coates said he thought Fay's show would be dangerous for the children because there wouldn't be enough adults to supervise them, and he advised Taylor to refuse to rent it for that purpose.

Coates told the inquest he considered Fay to be solely responsible for the tragedy, because "after the hall is taken, I consider that I have nothing to do with it. I take no more interest in the transaction until I receive the money in payment."

Coroner: "You consider that the responsibility rested on Mr. Fay?"

Coates: "I considered that it did not rest on me, but upon the entertainer."

Coroner: "Someone must be responsible for seeing to the safety of such a large number of children."

Coates: "I think so."

Coroner: "Then you satisfied yourself that Mr. Fay was responsible?"

Coates: "Yes. I asked him what staff he had, and he said that he had an ample one."

Coroner: "When was that?

Coates: "When he first asked me about the Saturday afternoon entertainment, on the Thursday. I suggested the advisability of not using the gallery."

Coroner: "Why?"

Coates: "Because it is rarely used for children's entertainments. As far as I recollect the gallery had not been opened for the use of children on a

Saturday, except persons who have had the whole hall for a week. I never knew of such a case as Mr. Fay's."

Coroner: "Has this arisen from the idea that the gallery would be dangerous?"

Coates: "Yes. I think that the idea was that it would be difficult to look after the children, as probably the entertainment would not be able to proceed in consequence of their being uproarious."

Decisions of the inquests:

The Bishopwearmouth jury ruled that the children died by suffocation "from the partial closing of a door on the landing, fixed in its position by a bolt in the floor, but by whom there is not sufficient evidence to show."

The jury blamed Fay for "not providing sufficient caretakers and assistants to preserve order in the hall on that afternoon" and recommended the fateful door be removed "at once."

The jury added it did not blame the caretaker, Mr. Graham, but recommended Taylor tell him to show future renters of the hall all its exits and entrances.

The Monkwearmouth jury agreed the children died by suffocation because of the bolted door and also agreed there wasn't enough evidence to show who did it, but it did say it was a neglect of duty for the hall-keeper Graham not to tell Fay and his assistants about the door. They also submitted the following answers to their coroner's questions:

Question 1: Upon whom rested the legal duty or responsibility of taking proper precautions for the preservation of the lives of the children whilst within and on leaving the Victoria Hall? Did this responsibility devolve on the proprietor of the hall, his agent, or caretaker, or on Fay or Coates, or either of them?

Answer: Fay and Coates.

Question 2: What was the particular neglect of duty (if any) which led to the loss of the children's lives? Was it in omitting to provide a sufficient staff of attendants to keep order within the gallery and on the staircase during the departure of the children?

Answer: It was.

Question 3: Was the staff provided sufficient for the purpose if the fatal door had not existed?

Answer: No.

Question 4: Was the caretaker's omission to inform Fay and his assistants of the existence of that door a neglect of duty?

Answer: Yes.

Question 5: Was his further omission to reverse the position of the door and bolt it securely to the floor against the wall on the outer side of the landing (although he passed it twice during the performance, the last time about 4 p.m.) a further neglect of duty?

Answer: Yes.

Question 6: Were the directors of the Victoria Hall Company, Limited, justified in erecting such an unusual door with such peculiar fastenings in such an unusual position without instructing the caretaker to call the special attention of strangers taking the hall to that door and its fastenings?

Answer: No.

Question 7: Were parents (or relatives having charge) of the children justified in allowing children of tender age to go alone or in company of other young children to a probably crowded public entertainment without first satisfying themselves that some grown-up persons were intending to take charge of them?

Answer: No.

Question 8: "Were the masters of the various schools justified in allowing the children under their charge to be canvassed by Fay or their teachers, and the attendance of the children in effect secured by free tickets being given to teachers, without some arrangement being made for proper supervision and control of the children by their teachers when at the entertainment?

Answer: No.

The Coroner, after reading the verdict, asked the jury if they had decided whether the negligence of Fay and Coates was of a culpable character.

The Foreman replied that the jury did not go that length.

The jury also recommended school children not be encouraged to attend "entertainments, treats, or excursions, except under proper supervision or control."

And it also made a recommendation that laws be passed immediately to force all proprietors of any buildings of public assembly to make sure all their exits have doors that open outwards. This is the origin of today's "push-bar" emergency doors that can be seen in all theatres, religious buildings, offices and other such structures today.

With the benefit of hindsight, and by examining the event through a modern lens, the key person to blame here is Mr. Fay, the entertainer. He had performed many times before throughout England, so he had experience with large crowds of children. At Sunderland, he enticed them to the show with "prizes" and then deliberately made them compete with each other for them, so he would have known the frenzy this would have caused. He didn't hire enough people for crowd control. He didn't give the people he did hire clear instructions on how to get the children out.

At the end of his show, Fay didn't make clear to the children in the balcony where they could get their prizes. He should have said loudly and clearly that there was a man coming up to them with some prizes and once they were gone, there would be no more. Fay also should have asked them to leave by the doors that led outside. He should have asked them to leave slowly and carefully. He should have asked the few adults up in the balcony to keep an eye on the children around them. He should have recruited them to guide the children outside. He did none of this.

Fay needed to communicate much better with everyone at the hall that day, and not just assume they and the children would know what to do.

Whoever bolted the door to the floor is less at fault. It was probably a misguided effort to control the crowd, to prevent chaos, rather than anything negligent. Without the frenzy triggered by Fay's prizes, it would not have been an issue, though the jurors were quite right to demand its removal. If there had ever been a fire upstairs, a similar disaster could have happened.

5

Space Shuttle Challenger

By 1984, space flight in the United States had grown fairly routine. The first space shuttle, Columbia, had launched three years earlier to great fanfare but its subsequent missions of satellite deployment and research did not capture the public imagination as much, and public excitement about the missions was waning.

To keep interest up, and to inspire interest in math, science and space exploration, the National Aeronautics and Space Administration decided to create the Teacher in Space Project. The idea was to put an actual teacher into space and have him or her return to classrooms to give lessons about the mission.

The project was announced by President Ronald Reagan on August 27th, 1984 and more than 11,000 teachers applied. Out of those, NASA chose Christa McAuliffe, a social studies teacher at Concord High School in Concord, New Hampshire, to go into space on the Space Shuttle Challenger January 22nd, 1986.

After more than a year of training and preparation, McAuliffe was one of a crew of seven astronauts ready for the six-day mission to deploy two devices – a tracking and data-relay satellite and a tool to monitor Halley's Comet, which was due to pass by Earth a couple weeks later, on February 9th. McAuliffe was also scheduled to give televised lessons from space to school children around the United States.

But when it came to launch day, NASA ran into a series of problems. Far from being the easy-launch-and-return space vehicle that designers had hoped for, the four space shuttles – Columbia, Challenger, Discovery and Atlantis – were prone to myriad problems and glitches that kept them indoors or on the launch pad.

McAuliffe's mission was delayed, firstly because a previous mission was late, and then due to bad weather at the Florida launch site, then bad weather in west Africa where the emergency landing strips were, then because of a faulty exterior latch handle, and finally because of more bad weather in Florida.

The last-minute unpredictable weather delays were enormously frustrating for NASA decision-makers because they would come at the end of a very long, deliberate and meticulous approval process that took several months.

Prior to every space shuttle launch, NASA began a Shuttle Flight Readiness Review. It was a carefully planned, step-by-step series of checklists and meetings to make sure all shuttle components are ready for each mission.

The process began at the lowest level – Level IV – when contractors to NASA certified in writing that the shuttle components they built and were responsible for were in good working order.

The contractors then sent these certifications to their Level III NASA project managers which were then gathered and reviewed by a panel at the Kennedy Space Center in Florida, chaired by the Center Director. Finally, the Director verified the components were indeed ready.

The next step in the process – Level II – was the Certification of Flight Readiness. Here, each program certified that it had manufactured, assembled, tested and checked each element to make sure it met the required standard. The certifications were then sent for Level I review.

At Level I, a Mission Management Team was established for each mission, which assumed overall responsibility 48 hours prior to the scheduled launch date, and did not relinquish it until the mission was officially complete, well after landing. The team met 24 hours before the launch – a gathering called an L-1 – and its agenda included making sure all work was complete, that the emergency landing sites were ready and the weather was acceptable.

It was at an L-1 meeting at noon on January 27th that the Challenger launch was scrubbed and a new launch scheduled for 9:38 a.m. on the 28th. The L-1 officials noted the weather forecast for the next morning was for unusually low temperatures – possibly in the low 20s Fahrenheit – and they asked engineers to report on how that could affect a launch the next day. No critical issues were immediately identified, so they continued with the countdown and fueling the external tank.

At 2:00 p.m. on the 27th, the L-1 team met once more. The issue of cold weather came up again, and managers were informed the freezing temperatures would affect things like the water drains, the eye wash and shower water and the fire suppression system. In response, the team decided to activate heaters in the shuttle but to proceed with the countdown and with fueling. As usual, team members were reminded to stay alert for problems and to report immediately any that might come up for review.

When Robert Ebeling, the man in charge of the shuttle's ignition system, heard the launch was proceeding, he was immediately concerned. Ebeling worked for Morton-Thiokol Inc., the company that made the shuttle's reusable solid rocket boosters, and he had known for years they shouldn't be used in cold weather.

In particular, Ebeling was concerned about the integrity of the O-rings, which were made of a putty-like substance used to seal sections of the boosters during their assembly on site at Kennedy Space Center.

In previous shuttle launches, the O-rings had proven barely reliable on ignition, allowing spurts of intensely hot gases to escape and scar the seals before the O-rings – both primary and secondary ones – could recover and reseal the joints. The phenomenon was called "blow by" because pressurized hot gasses would "blow by" the O-rings and torch the external fuel tank. Although "blow by" lasted only tiny fractions of a second, engineers at Thiokol rated the problem serious.

Thiokol managers, in consultation with NASA, eventually decided they needed to redesign the joints and O-rings and by January, 1986, had begun the process. But the redesign wasn't considered critical enough to ground all shuttle flights, so the Challenger mission was allowed to proceed.

As more shuttle missions took place, however, the Thiokol engineers noticed a trend – the lower the air temperatures at lift off, the worse the O-rings performed. In fact, at the launch with the previous lowest temperature of 53 degrees Fahrenheit – the Discovery mission on January 24th, 1985 – the O-ring damage was the worst ever recorded.

So when Ebeling and his colleagues heard NASA would proceed with the Challenger launch in freezing temperatures – far below any previous launch temperature – they knew they couldn't sit idle.

At about 2:30 p.m., Ebeling called an urgent meeting of his fellow Thiokol engineers to discuss the matter. The meeting lasted an hour and they all agreed the cold-weather O-ring data was worrisome, especially because no shuttle had ever been launched in such low temperatures.

Ebeling then called Allan McDonald, Thiokol's liaison for the solid rocket boosters at Kennedy Space Center, and told him that with temperatures forecast to be as low as 18 degrees Fahrenheit, engineers were worried about the O-rings. Ebeling asked McDonald for updated weather forecasts so the engineers could make some calculations.

McDonald got the latest forecast and told Ebeling NASA was predicting an overnight low of 22 degrees, rising to 26 at launch time at 9:38 a.m.

They both agreed the matter was serious, so McDonald told Ebeling to prepare some charts for a presentation and then he called Thiokol's vice-president of engineering, Bob Lund, to involve him in the discussions. Soon, a tele-conference call was set up for 5:45 p.m. to allow everyone to discuss this issue.

On the tele-conference, Thiokol engineers expressed their concerns about a cold-weather launch. Some NASA representatives interpreted their worries as a request for a delay, while others heard only doubts, without an express recommendation.

Still, the matter was deemed serious enough to hold a second tele-conference, this time with even more senior executives and with Ebeling's charts, which had just been prepared.

On the second call, one of Ebeling's engineering colleagues at Thiokol, Roger Boisjoly, made a memorable, passionate plea to halt the launch. Grabbing the charts, he told those assembled that cold O-rings react slower to the ignition, and that the coldest previous launch saw the most serious "blow by" damage. Extrapolating that data down to 22 or 26 degrees, he said, could cause the primary and secondary O-rings to fail, causing a massive explosion that would doom the shuttle and its astronauts.

One NASA executive in the room asked Boisjoly to "quantify" his concerns, meaning to show data that would support his concerns, but he conceded he had none. He repeated, however, the correlation between cold weather and "blow by" damage.

After Boisjoly's presentation, Lund, speaking on behalf of all the Thiokol engineers, declared their conclusion – the shuttle should not fly at temperatures below 53 degrees.

The recommendation infuriated George Hardy, the deputy director of science and engineering at NASA's Marshall Space Centre in Huntsville, Alabama, who told the others he was "appalled" at the conclusion. Just because there was some damage to the Discovery at 53 degrees didn't give nearly enough proof that cold weather was to blame, he said. Plus, there were other design elements that provided many other levels of safety, he added. None of the data presented seemed to change any of the basic engineering behind the design of the joint.

However, he did add that if the engineers truly were against a launch, he would not disagree.

Another shuttle program manager, Lawrence Mulloy, was outright sarcastic towards the engineers:

"My God, Thiokol. When do you want me to launch, next April?" he said.

The worries about the O-rings were nothing new to Mulloy. He had heard them for years but always considered them an acceptable flight risk. In fact, these concerns had come up six consecutive times on previous launches and he'd dismissed them each time.

Mulloy pointed out the shuttle had flown successfully 24 times under the current safety checklist, which had proven to be reliable. Adding another item to the checklist – namely "cold temperature" – would need to be carefully considered by staff, not done at the last minute.

"We need to consider this carefully before we jump to any conclusions," Mulloy said.

"Is it truly logical that we really have a system that has to be 53 degrees to fly?"

Mulloy's question infuriated Boisjoly, who slapped down photos of the Discovery's boosters after they launched in 53 degrees, showing considerable "blow by."

"How the hell can you ignore this?" he said.

With tempers rising, Joe Kilminster, the vice president of space boosters at Morton-Thiokol, and Lund join other Thiokol representatives in leaving the call to discuss the matter on their own. The others told Lund, an engineer by training, he should "put on his management hat" for the meeting. They went through cold-weather launch data – weighing evidence both for and against – and decided to proceed with a launch the following morning.

All, including Lund, agreed that there was a substantial margin of error for the O-rings – three times the previous worst case – and that even if the primary O-ring did not seal due to the cold, the secondary O-ring would. They said they were concerned about the low temperatures but the data about the O-rings were inconclusive.

The Thiokol reps then rejoined the call and gave their decision. Allan McDonald, the director of the solid rocket motor project at the company, still objected, and said if anything happened to the shuttle, he would not want to have to explain it to a board of inquiry. McDonald was told by others his concerns would be passed on but Thiokol's recommendation would stand.

Boisjoly and others were shocked, but they gave up arguing. They felt they had done all they could to prevent the launch – they argued their case, presented their data – but had to yield to their managers' prerogative to make the final decision on a launch.

George Hardy, the NASA director who said he was appalled at Thiokol's initial reluctance, then asked Kilminster to fax over his company's assent to the launch, which he did at 11:45 p.m., signing it himself. Just three hours earlier, Kilminster had been opposed.

Mulloy and another NASA manager then discussed other issues surrounding the launch with their bosses – ice build-up on the shuttle, the activities of some of the recovery ships – but did not mention the Thiokol engineers' concerns about the O-rings. Their call ended around midnight.

At 5 a.m. January 28th, Mulloy told William Lucas, the director of the Marshall Space Flight Center in Huntsville, Alabama, of the concerns about the O-rings but in the same breath said they were alleviated.

At 6:18 a.m. on the 28th, the crew was given a wake-up call but they were already up. For the next 90 minutes, they ate breakfast, got a weather briefing and put on their flight gear. They were driven to the launch pad at 8:03 a.m. and by 8:36 they were in their seats in Challenger. No one ever told them about the engineers' O-ring concerns.

Between 7 a.m. and 9 a.m., crews inspected the shuttle on the launch pad. They found the left-hand solid-rocket booster was 25 degrees Fahrenheit, with parts of it covered in ice, and the right one was as low as 8 degrees Fahrenheit, so the program manager decided to delay the launch until 11:38 a.m., to give the ice more time to melt.

At around 8 a.m., Lovingood told Jack Lee, the deputy director of the Marshall Space Flight Centre, of the O-ring concerns and of Thiokol's change of heart.

At 9 a.m., a top-level NASA management discussion was held and while they discussed ice conditions, they didn't talk about the effect of low temperatures on the O-ring seals.

At 10:30 a.m. ice crews notified the Mission Management Team that there was still ice on the left solid-rocket booster.

At 11:15 a.m. a final ice inspection was done and the shuttle's crew and all members of the launch team gave their "go" for launch.

At 11:38 a.m., the air temperature at the launch pad was recorded at 36 degrees Fahrenheit. NASA ignited the Challenger's solid rocket boosters and released its hold-down bolts with explosives, freeing the shuttle from the pad.

The shuttle was now doomed. Less than a second after liftoff, the massive internal pressure in the right-hand solid-rocket booster popped one of the joints outwards, ballooning the casing and allowing 5,000-degree gases to spray out. The primary O-ring filled the gap a split second later, but it was not pliable enough and failed again. This sealing-unsealing happened dozens of times in the next minute, eroding the quality of both the primary and secondary O-rings until they failed permanently.

The shuttle was given a momentary reprieve, however, when by chance aluminum oxides from the burned propellant sealed the joint in place of the O-ring. But then the shuttle was buffeted by a massive wind shear, which knocked out the temporary oxide seal. The fuel now had a consistent hole through which to burn, and it shot outward like a blowtorch.

Back on the ground, mission control scientists saw on their monitors that internal pressure in the right solid-rocket booster dropping, but they didn't immediately consider it a concern.

At 65 seconds post-launch, the flame began burning a hole in the much-larger external tank which was filled with liquid hydrogen, and it, too, began to leak. Its drop in pressure was also noted by the scientists. The shuttle's systems automatically started to compensate for the loss of thrust on one side, though to everyone in the shuttle and on the ground, the mission still seemed quite normal.

Among the millions watching the liftoff on TV were the skeptical engineers who fought until almost midnight the night before to prevent it. They thought if the O-rings were to fail, they'd do so almost immediately – right on the launch pad. But when they saw Challenger rise past the guidance tower and into the frigid blue sky they exhaled. Maybe everything will be OK after all, they said.

At this point, one of Boisjoly's friends turned to him and said "Oh, God. We made it. We made it."

At 73 seconds, at an altitude of 48,000 feet and at nearly twice the speed of sound, the rear strut holding the bottom of the right solid-rocket booster in place failed, and the shuttle jerked violently to the right. Pilot Michael J. Smith said "Uh oh," a split second before the hydrogen tank exploded and the shuttle disintegrated in a giant vapor plume. The solid rocket boosters continue on aimlessly, until they were sent an auto-destruct command.

The millions of TV viewers, including McAuliffe's own students, watching the launch around the world were initially perplexed, wondering if what they were watching was normal. But Boisjoly and his colleagues knew right away what happened. And they were sick with grief.

"Flight controllers here looking very carefully at the situation," said the NASA announcer at Kennedy Space Center, as the network TV cameras showed two solid rocket boosters zooming aimlessly in the clear blue sky. "Obviously a major malfunction."

Within minutes, the facts became clear. The shuttle was destroyed and the seven astronauts on board were dead.

The Presidential Commission on the Space Shuttle Challenger Accident was chaired by William Rogers, a former U.S. Secretary of State, vice-chaired by Neil Armstrong, the first person to walk on the moon.

The commission was succinct in declaring the physical cause of the accident: Hot gases leaking through a joint in the right-hand solid rocket booster during the propellant burn destroyed the O-rings, leading to a catastrophic explosion.

The commission found that the O-rings had long been a concern of engineers, well before the first space shuttle flight in 1981 At least one of those pre-1981 tests showed their design was flawed and could allow the burning gases to burst through the seals, leading to almost certain destruction of the shuttle.

Years before the Challenger tragedy, engineers at the Marshall Space Flight Centre in Alabama wrote to George Hardy, the manager of the Solid Rocket Booster project telling him the design was seriously flawed. In particular, one engineer said if the primary O-ring failed, the second one would be useless. But for whatever reason, Hardy did not pass on their concerns and the joint design was approved by NASA.

Even after the shuttle was flying, engineers' concerns about the O-rings mounted. After the second shuttle mission in November, 1981, crews found evidence of serious O-ring damage and forwarded their findings to the Marshall Space Flight Centre. Marshall management told the company that made the boosters, Morton-Thiokol, but not NASA itself.

As the missions progressed, the evidence of a design flaw kept mounting. More and more shuttle missions were showing "blow by" and fewer and fewer engineers were willing to keep silent about their fears the problem could lead to a catastrophe.

By 1985, both Marshall Space Flight Center and Morton-Thiokol agreed the joints needed to be reclassified as "Criticality 1" meaning their failure would destroy the shuttle. The companies then tasked their engineers to begin the process of redesigning them but they did not call for the shuttles to be grounded in the meantime.

The commission also delved deep into the decision-making process at NASA in order to find out why top-level managers decided to launch the Challenger when so many engineers had been opposed.

The results were damning. Even though it had been clear years before the Challenger disaster that the O-rings were not as secure as originally hoped, and were increasingly susceptible to failure the colder they were, top managers ignored or dismissed this evidence and even withheld it from their superiors.

"The decision to launch the Challenger was flawed," said the Rogers report. "Those who made that decision were unaware of the recent history of problems concerning the O-rings and the joint and were unaware of the initial written recommendation of the contractor advising against the launch at temperatures below 53 degrees Fahrenheit and the continuing opposition of the engineers at Thiokol after the management reversed its position."

The report said the decision makers did not clearly understand the shuttle was not safe to launch at that temperature. If they had known all the facts "it is highly unlikely that they would have decided to launch 51-L on January 28, 1986," it said.

A better decision-making system would have flagged the engineers' doubts about the O-rings and made sure they were brought to attention at the highest levels.

Part of the reason why NASA didn't have the information it needed was a propensity at the Marshall Space Flight Center to try to resolve serious problems internally rather than get outside advice. The commission said this was "altogether at odds with the need for Marshall to function as part of a system working toward successful flight missions, interfacing and communicating with the other parts of the system that work to the same end."

The Commission also concluded that managers at Morton-Thiokol agreed to the launch, despite earlier reservations, in order to "accommodate a major customer."

The commission made many recommendations to prevent a similar tragedy including the obvious one of improving the design of the solid rocket boosters, plus independent oversight of the process.

It also suggested making managers more accountable to the overall shuttle program, rather than to their own departments and companies.

The commission also recommended putting astronauts in management positions – something that had been common in the 1960s and 1970s but which had fallen out of favor – to ensure astronaut safety remained paramount when big decisions are made.

It also suggested that the flight crew commander from the shuttle mission, or a designated representative, should attend the critical Flight Readiness Review, prior to launch. If this had been done with the Challenger, the crew would have known about the O-ring problems at low temperatures and could have vetoed the decision to launch.

Looked at today, the essential communications failure at the centre of the Challenger disaster can be found in the fateful meeting of engineers and managers the night prior to launch, though its roots reach back years.

It was at this meeting that the program's top engineers confronted the programs top decision-makers with evidence that a cold-weather launch of the shuttle could be disastrous.

The engineers told their bosses the colder the weather, the worse the O-rings performed. Since January 28th, 1986 was going to be by far the coldest day for a shuttle launch ever, and since NASA had no test data to guess how the O-rings would perform at such temperatures, they begged for the launch to be delayed. And yet, the top brass OK'd the launch.

Were the managers just callous bureaucrats? Did they care only about meeting a schedule? Were they impatient due to the persistent delays?

The answers are certainly "no" to each question. Everyone in that room knew what would happen if the O-rings failed, and there's no evidence anyone was acting against the best interests of NASA.

The problem lies somewhere between what the engineers were saying and what the decision-makers heard.

Could it be that the engineers didn't make themselves clear? Quite possibly, yes.

Years after the disaster, an American statistician, Edgar Tufte, claimed the graph the engineers presented to the NASA decision-makers January 27th, 1986 that aimed to show the correlation between temperature and O-ring damage was confusing and hard to understand. It displayed tiny line diagrams of all 48 boosters used in shuttle launches, arrayed in chronological order like crayons in a box. Below them were the launch temperatures and tiny scribbles where they suffered O-ring damage. The information, including the writing, was densely packed.

Tufte, who coined the term "chartjunk" to describe useless information put on charts, said the graph utterly failed to convey the serious warning about the imminent disaster. He said the engineers should have presented a simple line graph, with temperature on one axis and the number of damaged O-rings per launch. If they had, the NASA decision-makers would have seen a very simple trend line that showed the colder the temperature, the more O-ring damage.

The graph was just one possible problem with the presentation. Another may have been the language the engineers used.

When Boisjoly, the Morton-Thiokol engineer, was asked for evidence showing the link between cold temperatures and O-ring damage beyond the circumstantial evidence in the graph, he replied he didn't have anything direct. But he was reported to have said "it was away from goodness in the current database."

"Away from goodness" is about as vague a term for "bad" as can be. This is the kind of language resorted to by people afraid to state things clearly. Boisjoly probably wanted to say definitively "the shuttle will be destroyed if you launch this morning," but he couldn't because he didn't have enough evidence. They found themselves restrained in what they wanted to say by a lack of supporting data.

Instead, Boisjoly and his fellow engineers should have turned the tables on their bosses. Rather than having to prove the launch would be dangerous, they should have demanded the decision-makers prove it would be safe. The top brass wouldn't have been able to, of course, and might have reached the same conclusion – more study of the O-rings was needed, and the shuttle launch should have been delayed until the temperatures were above 53 degrees Fahrenheit.

The lives of seven astronauts would have been saved and Christa McAuliffe would have taught her lessons from space.

6

USS Vincennes

On the morning of Sunday, July 3rd, 1988, Iran Air Flight 655 took off from Bandar Abbas, Iran, on a 28-minute flight south to Dubai, in the United Arab Emirates.

Iran was in the final stages of an eight-year war against Iraq that had already claimed about half a million lives but pilot Mohsen Rezaian wasn't worried about coming under fire. His Airbus 300 was one of 10 that would be taking off that day. His jet was to stay within an internationally recognized commercial air corridor across the Strait of Hormuz, a very narrow part of the Persian Gulf. It would go nowhere near Iraq or the vicious fighting on the front lines.

He knew, however, he would likely fly his 274 passengers and 15 other crew members over American navy ships, as the U.S. was patrolling the Strait to ensure that the flow of critical oil would continue out of the gulf. The Americans were officially neutral in the war but Iran long suspected – and their suspicions were largely true – that the U.S. was secretly aiding the Iraqis. The U.S. and Iran had not had diplomatic relations since the

1979 Iranian Revolution that overthrew the U.S.-backed Shaw and saw the seizure of 52 American hostages from the U.S. embassy in Tehran.

In the three days before Iran Air 655 took off, the Iranians had retaliated to Iraqi airstrikes by stepping up their attacks on merchant ships and moving two or three of their F-14s from Bushehr to Bandar Abbas. This move was spotted by the Americans, who alerted their ships in the Persian Gulf to be on the lookout for more aggressive Iranian behavior, especially as the July 4th holiday was coming up, and the Iranians might want to attack on a symbolic date.

Iran had been attacking neutral shipping with its warplanes, surface ships and small boats in and around the Strait for years. When the Americans responded by deploying its navy to escort commercial shipping, Iran laid six mine fields across the Persian Gulf and in the Gulf of Oman in an effort to sink US warships and stop convoy operations.

These minefields damaged a Kuwaiti oil tanker and a US Navy frigate, and the U.S. responded by destroying two abandoned Iranian oil platforms and sinking an Iranian frigate, plus three armed high-speed boats.

The morning the Iran Air jet took off, the USS Montgomery was on patrol in the northern portion of the Strait of Hormuz when it saw seven small Iranian gunboats – with mounted machine guns and rocket launchers – zooming towards a Pakistani merchant ship.

Shortly thereafter they were joined by six more, which all then threatened the big ship, in groups of three or four. The Montgomery reported hearing several explosions to the north. It then responded and so did the Vincennes, which launched one of its helicopters. The Iranians shot at the chopper, which returned fire.

The Iranians did not back off but instead buzzed around the area firing and racing around at high speed. Both the Vincennes and the Montgomery challenged the smaller boats, which were maneuvering erratically, actions the US command said it considered threatening and hostile.

Both the Montgomery and Vincennes pursued the small boats into Iranian waters and opened fire with shells. However, the Vincennes soon suffered a "foul bore" – a round that had jammed in the chamber – in one of its main guns and its captain, Will Rogers III, ordered his ship to perform a high-speed, sharp angle turn to keep its other gun trained on the most dangerous of small boats harassing it. It was successful, but the maneuver caused books and loose equipment on board to fall from desks and shelves, and the ship's lights to flicker.

After several minutes, the Vincennes had fired a total of 72 five-inch shells at the small boats.

This skirmish in the Gulf was unknown to Capt. Rezaian in the cockpit of his Iran Air Airbus. The Bandar Abbas control tower often warned pilots when there were hostilities in the vicinity but apparently did not do so in this case.

Nevertheless, immediately after takeoff, Rezaian did take one precaution. He followed Iranian protocol to ensure the Americans would not mistake his Airbus A300 for a military jet, by switching on his aircraft's transponder to broadcast the normal identification code for a civilian plane.

This was particularly important because Bandar Abbas was a joint military-civilian airport from which the Iranians had launched F-4 jets in support of an attack on American forces three months earlier, and from which Iran had launched several F-14 fighter aircraft just a week prior. Capt. Rezaian wanted to make sure the Americans did not confuse his civilian airliner with a military jet.

At 10:17 a.m. Iran time, Iran Air 655 took off and began flying over the gulf, making sure to stay well within the assigned 20-mile-wide commercial air corridor. He was to ascend to 14,000 feet, cruise for a few minutes, and then descend to land in the UAE. The crew was maintaining English-language radio contact with Iranian flight control.

The Iran Air jet immediately appeared on the radar of the Vincennes, which had just broken off its firefight with the Iranian speedboats. However, the Vincennes's identification designation supervisor erroneously detected a Mode II signal, called a "squawk," from the airplane, which identified it as a military aircraft, rather than the civilian Mode III squawk it was actually sending out.

There was a quick discussion on board the Vincennes about whether the signal was from a military or commercial flight. One officer said it was probably still a commercial aircraft, despite the military squawk, but others disagreed, saying it was likely an F-14. The Airbus was then labeled "unidentified assumed hostile" even though the Vincennes picked up the correct civilian squawk code a moment later. This change was not passed onto the head officers.

This wasn't the only aircraft on the Vincennes's radar. The ship had already been tracking a real Iranian military aircraft – a Lockheed P-3 Orion used for maritime surveillance – about 60 nautical miles to its northwest, which Capt. Will Rogers III suspected might be scouting the area providing targeting information for an imminent attack.

Because of the perceived need to coordinate a response to the escalating situation, Captain Rogers was given command of the Montgomery and another US ship the Sides, which was also nearby.

Captain Rogers's crew checked immediately to see if this mystery plane's departure corresponded to a commercial airline schedule and the answer was no (the flight was 27 minutes late). And while it was within a known commercial air corridor, it was off the centre line by three to four miles, something American officers considered unusual.

Capt. Rogers had very little time to find out the plane's intentions – if hostile, it would be in firing range within about five minutes. So he ordered his crew to warn the mystery plane via civilian and military channels to identify itself and change course. He sent a total of seven warnings over the next few minutes.

The first warning on a military channel was:

"Unidentified Iranian aircraft on course 203, speed 303, altitude 4000, this is U.S. Naval warship, bearing 205, 40 miles from you. You are approaching U.S. Naval warship operating in international waters. Request you state your intentions."

The first warning on the civilian channel was:

"Unknown aircraft on course 206, speed 316 position 2702N/05616E you are approaching US Naval warship. Request you remain clear."

The Iran Air flight didn't respond to any of the warnings, which should not have been surprising. It had no capability to pick up military frequencies and the civilian-channel warnings could have been directed at any commercial jet in the area. The Vincennes did broadcast the speed of the jet it was warning, but listed its ground speed, not the airspeed, which was 50 knots different, so the Airbus crew might have thought the Americans were hailing another jet.

The Iran Air was in constant English-language contact with aircraft control officials but the Vincennes, despite all the high-tech equipment on board, did not have a radio capable of picking up normal civilian aviation frequencies, except the one for emergencies. It also did not attempt to contact the Iran Air via air traffic controllers.

When the Iran Air was just 28 miles away, Capt. Rogers told his commander that he had a closing Iranian F-14 which he would "engage" at 20 nautical miles if it didn't turn away, and asked for "concurrence" to do so.

The Commander agreed, but told the Vincennes to issue a warning before firing.

At a distance of 20 nautical miles, Capt. Rogers decided to keep up communication attempts and to emit fire-control radar at it, so it knew it had been spotted. Military jets have radar warning equipment and will know immediately when they have been "locked" onto prior to being fired on. Commercial aircraft normally do not, and their pilots would have had no idea they were being signaled in this way.

The jet continued its climb past 10,000 feet without reacting to the U.S. radar or the warnings from the Vincennes.

When the plane was about 15 nautical miles away, Capt. Rogers was told by one of his officers that the jet had suddenly started descending, exactly like a military jet would on an attack run. This, again, was false. The Airbus continued to ascend normally.

The officer who reported the descent was simply passing on what he was hearing from at least one petty officer but, critically, he made no effort to confirm the information with the equipment in front of him. Had he done so, he would have seen that the petty officer was wrong and the jet was in fact ascending, not descending.

So, with the jet now 10 miles away, Capt. Rogers, having sent several more warnings on civilian and military channels, was presented with the following information:

1.   His ship had just engaged several hostile Iranian boats that had been swarming around him.

2.   An "unidentified assumed hostile" jet had just taken off from a military airfield towards his ship.

3.   This jet was not responding to requests for identification and was not radiating definitive electronic signals.

4.   His ship's warnings to the jet went unanswered.

5.   If he didn't fire the missiles in the next few seconds, it would be too late.

Capt. Rogers made his decision – shoot the jet down. He turned the firing key and two missiles streaked off their rails and blew the Airbus out of the sky at an altitude of 13,500 feet, eight miles from the Vincennes. All 290 people from six nations, including 66 children, were killed.

From first detection to the intercept, the elapsed time was seven minutes and eight seconds.

U.S. jets swooped over the crash area and spotted dozens of bodies floating in the water along with a lot of debris.

The Vincennes and several Iranian helicopters converged on the crash site. The Vincennes offered to help but got no response.

The Iranian government and much of the international community were understandably outraged by the actions of the U.S. Navy. The Iran Air was in a regular commercial corridor on a regularly scheduled flight. It was squawking a commercial frequency and was ascending normally when it was shot down.

The American military, while rejecting any blame for the tragedy, ordered an immediate investigation, which was headed by Admiral William Fogarty.

Fogarty's investigation maintained the American stance that its military was not to blame, though he probably faced enormous political pressure to avoid assigning any kind of blame to Americans, so this statement must be viewed in that light.

Captain Rogers acted prudently, based on the information available to him in such a short timeframe and while fighting Iranian speedboats, said

Fogarty. There were just minutes and 40 seconds between when the jet was identified as a possible threat to his decision to shoot it down.

Fogarty also said the Iranians Iran must share responsibility for the tragedy by allowing one of its airliners to fly over a military skirmish – again, he may not have been able to say anything else.

The Captain was blameless, Fogarty said, because he based his decision to fire his missiles at the jet on the following information:

- The aircraft had taken off from a joint civilian/military airport.

- It was not in the middle of the assigned commercial flight corridor.

- It appeared at one point to veer toward the USS Montgomery.

- It was reported to be descending and increasing speed and closing fast.

- It was not responding to warnings.

- It was initially reported to be squawking a military ID code.

- It would not be possible to see the jet until it was too late.

- It was flying at the same time US and Iranian forces were shooting at each other.

- Warnings had been issued about increased Iranian military activity, especially for July 4th.

- An Iranian surveillance aircraft was already in the air.

- Iranian military jets had earlier flown during naval fighting.

However, Fogarty admitted there were some other, equally unavoidable, facts that raised some serious questions about the competency of the officers on board the Vincennes.

- At no time did the flight actually descend before it was hit with missiles.

- While it was not exactly in the center of the flight corridor – 3.7 nautical miles northwest of it – it was still in the assigned airway.

- The flight squawked Mode III the entire flight, not Mode II.

- The Mode II received was probably from another, military, aircraft at the airport but assigned to IA 655 for 90 seconds in error.

Fundamentally, said Fogarty, the American commander based his decision to shoot the jet down on some information was horribly wrong, most crucially the assertion that the jet was diving and accelerating towards the Vincennes. The ship's computers were reviewed after the disaster and investigators found they never once indicated such a flight path – it ascended normally, just as a commercial jet would be expected to do.

So, if Rogers was not to blame, how could well-trained and experienced navy officers at properly functioning computers tell their captain a jet was descending when it was ascending?

Fogarty suspected the answer lay in a theory called "scenario fulfillment" where people under pressure will carry out a well-rehearsed training protocol because it's what they've learned to do, rather than think for themselves and look for alternate information.

Fogarty wrote there were two crew members in particular on the Vincennes who became convinced the jet was an Iranian F-14 from the moment it was erroneously identified as squawking Mode II. One of these officers appeared to him to have "distorted data flow in an unconscious attempt to make available evidence fit a preconceived scenario."

Adding to the time pressure were the sudden, severe movements of the ship as it veered to confront the small boats buzzing around it. This, combined with the sound of guns firing, gear falling off shelves and flickering lights all heightened the tension on board, Fogarty said.

After going to great lengths to exonerate his fellow naval officers of any blame, the problem for Fogarty then was to make some recommendations on how to avoid making a similar disastrous decision.

First he pointed out the things that could not or should not be changed:

- It really doesn't matter what code the jet is squawking, since a pilot on a suicide mission or a sneak attack would want to squawk a civilian code anyway to avoid suspicion.

- Having naval officers learn commercial flight schedules would be pointless. At this time in 1988, there were more than 1,000 flights per week in the Persian Gulf area and it would have been impossible to update and maintain such a list. Besides, commercial flights are often late – such as this one was – or cancelled at the last moment.

- Visual identification of all jets in a radius around U.S. Navy ships would be impossible.

Then he recommended that the chief naval officer should order a study be done on how stress affects those on board navy ships, especially when it comes to decision making and dealing with high-tech equipment. The study should also try to find the ideal psychological profile for working in such an environment, and – by implication – find out what kind of people should not work there.

Fogarty also recommended telling all Persian Gulf nations and airlines operating in the area to tell their pilots to ascend to at least 25, 000 feet before crossing the Persian Gulf. At that altitude, all aircraft could be considered non-threatening, regardless of whether they were military or commercial, or their squawk frequency, speed or trajectory. Below that level, the US Navy would be forced to consider any jet, even commercial ones (they could be flown by suicide pilots), as a potential threat. Any aircraft that couldn't reach that altitude would have to make sure to contact U.S. ships in the area by radio before coming within five miles of them.

He also said radio warnings from US naval craft to airplanes should be standardized because he felt the warnings used by the Vincennes and other ships in the Middle East at the time were ambiguous because they did not clearly identify to pilots exactly which aircraft the ship was attempting to contact.

Therefore, he suggested the following standard warning:

"Unidentified air/surface contact squawking _____ at (reference to geographical point), at _____ altitude, on course _____ and speed _____, you are approaching a U.S. warship operating in international waters. Your identity is not known/your intentions are unclear (use of one or both statements would be OK), you are standing into danger and may be subject to United States defensive measures. Request you alter your course immediately to remain clear of me."

In the final analysis, the communications problems in this incident began with the misidentification of the Iran Air jet as military, rather than commercial. This failure of Vincennes's detection equipment would not been an entirely unusual occurrence, so it was negligent of the US officers not to strive to confirm the signal.

It was also negligent of the American officers not to double check all the other information given to them by their colleague who was claiming the jet was descending and picking up speed. Upon hearing the initial report of a jet approaching on an attack profile, Capt. Rogers should have asked other officers to confirm it. Rogers said he had no reason not to believe them, but that's not the issue. As suggested in the Cockpit Resource Management plan mentioned in Chapter 1, crew members should talk to each other – out loud – about what they're seeing, and what they're doing, to eliminate confusion. If a second or third set of eyes had examined the ship's data, they would have seen the jet was climbing peacefully and the disaster may never have happened.

The American refusal to accept any blame in this incident is callous in the extreme, but perhaps understandable given the diplomatic mood of the time. The U.S. government never apologized to anyone for shooting a civilian jet full of passengers out of the air. It did, however, send notes of regret along with $131.8 million to the Iranians -- $300,000 per wage-earning victim and $150,000 for every non-wage-earner, plus $70 million, which was roughly the replacement cost of an Airbus – to settle a lawsuit. The U.S. also paid compensation to the families of all the non-Iranian victims.

The best way to have prevented the disaster was for the United States and Iran to have agreed beforehand that all commercial jets should fly over the Persian Gulf at an altitude of at least 25,000 feet. That's because it was the only sure way the Americans could have ruled them out as threats.

The Americans were right that if the Iranians wanted to launch a sneak attack on a U.S. ship, they would want to disguise their aircraft as a commercial jet – indeed it could actually have been a commercial jet a la September 11th, 2001 – by squawking a civilian code and staying in a designated flight path.

At 25,000 feet, even a military jet loaded with bombs and missiles would not be able to harm a U.S. Navy frigate at that height.

7

The Rushtons

Saturday, January 5th was a typically chilly winter day in northwest England when Stewart Rushton, 51, decided to take his nine-year-old son Adam out for an afternoon fishing trip at Morecambe Bay.

They parked their red Suzuki 4x4 near the beach and donned waders before walking out onto the vast expanse of beach, exposed at low tide, to look for shellfish to use for bait. They left their fishing gear in their car.

A short time later, the weather suddenly changed for the worse. Thick fog rolled in, enveloping them, and suddenly they found themselves standing on a rapidly shrinking sand bar ankle deep in water. When Stewart turned around, he realized to his horror he didn't know which way the beach was, and the tide was coming in fast.

He and his son walked one way for a while, then another, before he realized he'd have to call for help on his cell phone. The water was getting deeper.

His first call, at 2:19 p.m., was to his wife, Joy. He said they were enveloped in thick fog and she should call the coast guard right away, which she did.

The rescue crews knew to treat this call with the utmost urgency. For hundreds of years, Morecambe Bay has been known as a death trap. It is shaped like a funnel, so the incoming tide rushes in fast, pushing the water level up 11 yards in some cases.

But there's no obvious danger most of the time. At very low tides, about 120 square miles of beach is exposed, luring fishermen like the Rushtons out to compete with sea birds for the stranded mussels and clams. And until modern times, the temporary disappearance of the ocean also made the mudflats tempting for travelers looking for a shortcut to the north side of the bay, six and a half miles away. For many years, there was a regular horse-drawn caravan service between the two points.

But the bay's calm can be deceiving. Crossings had to be timed precisely and be led by experienced guides. Those who didn't obey the schedules were often swept to their deaths when the tides came in. The flooding can rush in faster than a man can walk, and seawater can surge along channels in the sand.

As recently as 1995, a local town councilor, who was an experienced hiker, vanished while strolling off Walney Island, at the northern tip of Morecambe Bay. He was trapped by the tide and his body wasn't recovered until two weeks later.

It's unknown exactly how many people have died in Morecambe Bay but there's a memorial in a nearby churchyard to 140 of its victims. The danger of the area has not been forgotten by the locals who have put up signs along the beaches warning of the risk. It's quite possible the Rushtons walked directly past one of these signs.

When the emergency call came in, four coastguard teams raced to the scene, joined by many local volunteers, an RAF helicopter, two mountain rescue teams and police officers. They called Stewart to ask for clues to his location, but he was so disoriented he couldn't give them any useful information.

The emergency operator kept calling him back – Rushton did not stay on the phone very long each call to conserve his phone's battery power – as water level rose up past his knees and then his hips. He could hear the boat engines and emergency sirens in the distance and called for help, but the rescuers couldn't determine where his shouts were coming from.

At 2:56 p.m., Stewart told rescuers the water was up to his neck, and so he put his son on his shoulders and handed him the phone.

"My daddy's all right," said Adam, though officials said they could hear his dad shouting for help from the rescuers he could hear in the distance but couldn't see. They told Adam to tell his dad that people were coming and would be there shortly.

Rescuers on shore, who included many relatives of the father and son, could also hear Rushton shouting, but couldn't pinpoint his location. They feared if they waded out into the water they would get lost, too.

Rushton's son-in-law Richard Creary was one of those who had rushed down to the beach to help. He said the visibility was no more than 50 yards. A family friend, Michael Burns, honked his car horn to give the pair an idea of the direction of the beach, to no avail.

At 3:02 p.m., officials made another call to Rushton, who acknowledged he could hear emergency sirens.

At 3:09, officials made another call, which was answered, but they didn't hear any voices, just the sound of water.

At 3:11, they made one last call, but could not make a connection.

By 3:15, investigators figured, the father and son were probably dead.

After the tide receded the next morning, a team of 100 searchers quickly found their bodies – Stewart was a mile and a half from the shore and Adam was a mile further away on the coast.

Two family members of the Rushtons had to be rescued, too, during their desperate search.

A transcript of the phone conversations between Rushton and the coast guard was made, but never released publicly because officials said it was too "distressing."

A few months later, an inquest was held into the deaths but the coroner, Ian Smith, never released his entire report. He did, however, make some comments to the local media.

Smith blamed Rushton for being "reckless" for walking onto a beach well known for similar kinds of drownings, according to a story by the Guardian newspaper.

"I believe he was very careless as to his own safety and that of course means he was careless about his son's safety," said Smith in his report, according to the Guardian.

"He took a risk he knew he was taking, walking out into those conditions. The price he paid was the ultimate price."

Raymond Porter, a Queen's guide to the sands and an expert on the area, said over the years hundreds of people had died in the estuary, which he described as "very dangerous," according to the Guardian.

He added that with such poor visibility that day no one should have attempted to walk out on to the beach, the paper said.

Ian Smith, the coroner, has not made his records available in this case, saying "coroner's records are not available to the general public." This is unhelpful, to say the least, and is a good example of how to reduce the information available to those concerned with preventing future tragedies. This policy should be reversed.

Smith's official ruling, as reported by the news media, was that Rushton died from "misadventure" and his son died by "accident."

But for Smith, the case ended there. According to news reports, he made no recommendations about how to prevent further deaths – which is often why inquests are called in the first place. Smith simply blamed the victims here.

"I believe he was very careless as to his own safety, his son's safety, and, more indirectly, the safety of rescuers," said Smith, as quoted by the Telegraph newspaper during the inquest.

"We are all responsible for our own safety. It is up to us not to get into situations that require us to be rescued."

It is true that once the Rushtons were caught in the fog, their fate was probably sealed. The only way out would have been to guess at the correct direction towards the beach and run. Neither Rushton nor his would-be rescuers could see more than 50 yards in any direction and the water was rapidly rising. Shouting did no good, because the thick fog banks reflected and echoed their voices, making auditory triangulation impossible. Strong lights would not have penetrated the fog either. Even the heat-seeking equipment on the coast guard helicopter was useless – the crews could not distinguish between the sea and air, and never picked up any sign of humans. With no landmarks, cell phone contact was also useless. Emergency crews would have had to happen upon the unfortunate pair to find them.

Simply put, Stewart Rushton should not have wandered so far from shore. But was his death ultimately his own fault? If this event is looked at in isolation, yes. He probably knew full well the danger of the beaches. He may well have known of the 1995 death on the north side of the bay and likely heard of others from friends, family, the media or school teachers. He also probably walked past one of the signs along the bay that warned of rising tides and quicksand.

But if we look at this incident in the context of centuries of similar ones, however, the death of the Rushtons must be considered the fault of local officials. The history books of the area are filled with people time and again getting caught unaware by the tide and fog. The Rushtons were just two of more than a hundred – and perhaps far more – to die in this way. It is clear that relying on people to read beach signs and to heed local lore is not enough. The local officials should and could have done far more to prevent this tragedy. They, including the coroner, are blaming the victims.

The first thing officials should do is understand that their warnings about the dangers are not getting through to all people. Then they have to understand why that is, and the answer is their signs don't say what they want them to say.

What do the signs say? According to a newspaper article, one says:

"Beware. Fast rising tides. Quick sands. Hidden channels."

That's clearly not enough. The warning mentions nothing about why people should beware. Many might ask 'what's so bad about a rising tide?' In most parts of the world, the tide creeps in so slowly as to be noticeable only after a few minutes.

As for quicksand, most people never encounter it and so would have no experience with it. Some might think they could avoid it by stepping carefully.

And what's a hidden channel? Again, most people probably don't know. In fact, it's a lane of water that runs faster than that surrounding it.

Simply put, a sign such as this places too much onus on the reader to understand the meaning. It's unfair to beachgoers and it shows local officials do not understand the basic nature of human communication.

What could the signs say? How about:

"Fog, rising tides and quicksand in this area have killed more than 100 people. Stay close to shore at all times."

Or:

"Heavy fog can disorient you and lead to death by drowning."

Much more needs to be done than change the wording on the signs. Local officials should expect some people to not see them or not understand them, so they should be better prepared to help people who do go out at high tide.

One thing they could do is to put dozens of wood piles in a grid pattern in the mudflats, so that people who get lost need only travel a short distance before encountering one. The piles could be labeled according to the grid – with signs like B-32 – so that the lost person could tell the emergency crews by cell phone exactly where he or she is. And if the person didn't have a phone, the piles could have simple ladders to allow people to climb up out of the rising water for a few hours until it recedes or help arrives.

These are just some suggestions. There could be many more.

The coroner's decision to blame Rushton for the deaths of himself and his son was entirely unhelpful, because just two years after the Rushton tragedy, 19 Chinese "cockle pickers" died in much the same way, in almost the same area. They were part of a group of 30 who ventured out onto the Morecambe Bay mudflats searching for shellfish were washed to their deaths in similar circumstances. According to the Guardian newspaper, the area's member of parliament said the next day the rush of people to harvest shellfish had been a "tragedy waiting to happen."

Morecambe Bay is a tragedy waiting to happen. And until local officials understand that better communication will save lives, more people will die.

8

Omagh

Saturday, 15 August 1998 was the Catholic Feast of the Assumption and the main commercial district of Omagh, Northern Ireland was crowded with shoppers, as there were just two weeks to go before the school year began.

At about 2 p.m., not long before a carnival was scheduled to proceed up the streets, two men drove a red Vauxhall Cavalier around the city courthouse, circling the area looking for a parking spot. The first one they could find was about 300 yards away, on Market Street just outside S.D. Kells, a popular school-uniform specialist, where many mothers were trying new clothes on their children.

The men parked at 2:19 p.m. and walked away from the vehicle, which had been stolen two days before, and now contained about 500 pounds of fertilizer-based explosive with a Semtex trigger.

At 2:32 p.m., a man with a "thick northern country accent" phoned the Ulster Television newsroom to say:

"There's a bomb, courthouse, Omagh. Main street. Five hundred pounds. Explosion 30 minutes."

The caller then gave the code word "Martha Pope" to confirm he was from the Real Irish Republican Army, a radical splinter group furious with the main IRA that had begun peace talks/just signed peace deal with the British.

At 2:33 p.m., the TV station received a second warning:

"Bomb, Omagh town. Fifteen minutes."

At 2:34 p.m. a third call was made to the Samaritans, a private charity, in the town of Coleraine. It was:

"Am I through to Omagh? This is a bomb warning. It's going to go off in 30 minutes."

The caller also said the bomb was 200 yards from the courthouse and also gave the code word 'Martha Pope'.

The warnings were immediately passed onto the Royal Ulster Constabulary – the Northern Irish police force – who began evacuation procedures immediately.

But finding the bomb was rather more difficult. According to one of the warnings, it was within 200 or so yards of the courthouse, but there was no "Main Street" in Omagh, so they guessed the callers meant "High Street," the road in front of the courthouse.

So police began to cordon off High Street, moving people up the road onto Market Street, away from the courthouse and they then began to search the courthouse and its vicinity for a bomb.

At 3:10, a sizeable crowd had gathered along Market Street, patiently waiting for the all clear. Among them was a group of Spanish students spending the day in Omagh with their new local friends.

There was little panic. People in Northern Ireland were somewhat used to such scares. Most in the crowd on Market Street either thought this would be declared a hoax or false alarm and their day would resume shortly, or if there were a bomb and if it did explode, they were far enough away from it.

And then the bomb exploded right among them, spewing shrapnel into the crowd and blasting the front off S.D. Kells and killing several people inside.

The blast shredded some people and tore limbs off others, while the intense heat burned many more. Further away, people were cut by flying glass and deafened from the sound.

The blast was so powerful it ripped up the pavement, rupturing a water line, sending a geyser of water that washed some of the dead and injured down the street.

Twenty-one people were killed instantly and more than 200 were injured, many critically. Eight more died in the hours and days afterward.

Among the dead were Avril Monaghan, 30, who was shopping at S.D. Kells and who was about to give birth to twins, along with her 18-month-old daughter Maura and her mother Mary Grimes. Monaghan's twins were killed, too.

Also killed was Rocio Abad Ramos, a 23-year-old Spanish woman who was guiding the group of Spanish and Irish children on a field trip when she heard about the bomb threat. In an effort to steer the children away from the bomb, she inadvertently guided them towards it. Four of the kids died with her – three 12-year-old boys and an eight-year-old boy – and several others were seriously wounded.

It was the deadliest terrorist act ever in the history of The Troubles, the violent resistance to British rule of Northern Island.

Suspicions for the bombing fell almost immediately on a group calling itself the Real Irish Republican Army, and those suspicions were soon confirmed when the group released a startling statement two days later to a Dublin newspaper, saying it was sorry.

The group claimed its targets were meant to be "commercial," adding "we offer our apologies to these civilians."

The RIRA said it wasn't ultimately to blame because it issued three separate warnings about the bomb, all with 40-minute notice – plenty of time for the police to evacuate the area. It also said the police blundered by assuming the bomb was near the courthouse when it wasn't.

"Each time the call was made it was very clear and the people talked back. The location was 300-400 yards from the courthouse. At no time was it said it was near the courthouse," the RIRA statement said.

"Despite media reports, it was not our intention at any time to kill any civilians...It was a commercial target, part of an ongoing war against the Brits...We offer apologies to the civilians.

The Northern Ireland Secretary at the time, Mo Mowlam, called the apology a "pathetic attempt to apologise for and excuse mass murder."

There were several criminal prosecutions but there were no guilty pleas and none of the subsequent trials ended in convictions, so there was no further insight into why the RIRA blundered so badly in its communication with the police.

Three years after the bomb, police ombudsman Nuala O'Loan was asked to look into allegations the Royal Ulster Constabulary had received tips in the days and weeks before the explosion, and had made mistakes in the subsequent investigation. O'Loan concluded the RUC should have followed up an anonymous warning of an unspecified attack on Omagh, and she criticized the mishandling of documents related to a tip from an informant three days before.

But neither the criminal trials nor the ombudsman's report focused on the main miscommunication at the heart of the attack – the poorly worded bomb warnings issued by the RIRA.

It appears the terrorists wanted their warnings to achieve two things – to destroy "commercial" shops along a busy street, and to terrify the population but not kill them.

Many believe the terrorists deliberately confused the police including the RUC Chief Constable Ronnie Flanagan.

"It was a totally inaccurate warning. To say there was a bomb planted at the courthouse and as my officers evacuated and searched that area, for a bomb to detonate 400 yards down the road. It's difficult to come to any other conclusion."

Flanagan also said this during an interview with BBC2 on August 16th, 1998.

"I can come to no other conclusion in that this was absolutely deliberate. We've had success in the past either through intercepting these vehicles before they arrive at their intended destination, or reaching them very soon after they have arrived so that we've been able to disrupt them, and I have no doubt that these people decided to give deliberately vague and misleading warnings to prevent us disrupting the explosive devices. I can come to no conclusion other than that these people intended the bloody murder that resulted from their actions."

If the terrorists had given a specific address where the car was parked, or even the name of the store it was parked in front of, the police would have found it right away and no lives likely would have been lost. So, why didn't they? Did they mean to confuse the police?

Despite the assertions of the police in this matter, it seems unlikely the terrorists actually meant to kill so many people.

Firstly, it was contrary to their modus operandi of spreading panic and keeping the hated RUC on their toes, but of limiting deaths to the police, the military and their supporters.

Secondly, the RIRA sent out an unprecedented apology two days later rather than boasting about their cleverness. In terrorist circles, issuing an apology must be considered humiliating.

Thirdly, the RIRA would have known killing so many innocent people – Catholics and Protestants (and a Mormon), adults and children – would set even their most ardent supporters against them, hurting their cause, such as it was. And in fact this is what happened. The bombing unleashed overwhelming international disgust and outrage, and spurred on the peace process. Within six years, the main IRA group – the Provisional IRA – agreed to a ceasefire, which still holds today, though the Real IRA is not part of the deal, and it continues to launch occasional attacks.

The terrorists' big blunder – besides the criminally negligent act of parking a car bomb on a busy street – was in assuming they would be understood. They failed to make sure the most important information go through to the police clearly – the location of the car.

When something as important as people's lives are at stake, it's critical that information be conveyed simply and clearly. Also, the listener should be asked to repeat the information back, out loud, so both people know the message has got through.

If the terrorists weren't sure of the address, they could have given out the make, colour and model of the car. That would have ruled out 99 per cent of the vehicles on the streets of Omagh, regardless of the address.

If the terrorists had thought more about what they were doing (ideally they wouldn't have assembled the bomb in the first place) their warning could have gone like this:

"There's a red Vauxhall Cavalier with a 500-pound bomb inside parked on Market Street in front of S.D. Kells. It will explode in 30 minutes."

Instead, the first warning was:

"There's a bomb, courthouse, Omagh. Main street. Five hundred pounds. Explosion 30 minutes."

Speaking simply and clearly when lives are at stake is a concept perhaps lost on terrorists who don't value human life very much. But their apology indicated they did have a tiny bit of compassion in their hearts so they should have had the decency to take more care with their warning. Instead, they gave out the wrong street and only a vague notion of the location of the bomb, and 29 people are dead because of it.

9

Fukushima

On March 11, 2011, at 2:46 p.m. seismic sensors detected the largest earthquake ever to strike Japan, 43 miles off the Oshika peninsula, measuring 9.0 on the Richter scale.

The earthquake was an undersea megathrust that sent powerful tsunami waves crashing into Japanese cities, towns and villages, some up to 133 feet high and some sending water up to six miles inland.

About 130,000 buildings were destroyed and nearly one million were damaged. The shockwaves and surging water destroyed roads, railways, harbors, schools, hospitals and devastated entire neighborhoods in the worst disaster to hit Japan since the end of World War II. Thousands were killed and injured.

At the Fukushima Daiichi Nuclear Power Plant on the east coast of Japan the scope of the offshore earthquake was immediately recorded by its sensors and its three operating reactors were automatically shut down (three others were already shut down for maintenance). Auxiliary diesel generators kicked in to provide power to the plant, most importantly to keep the super-hot reactors from overheating.

About 30 seconds after the automatic shutdown, the plant began to shake hard. It kept shaking for about 50 seconds, lifting, sinking and shaking the plant's buildings and pathways, causing some significant interior damage but not affecting critical operations.

The first tsunami wave hit the plant at around 3:30 p.m. It demolished the power grid in the area, and then swamped the rooms holding the emergency generators, knocking the plant's backup power off line. More waves washed into the plant, peaking at 3:37 p.m.

Without coolant, the three operating reactors quickly began overheating.

The plant workers responded immediately to the emergency but were severely hindered by the damage caused by the arrival of the ocean. The waves destroyed or washed away buildings, vehicles, heavy machinery, oil tanks and gravel. Seawater swamped all the buildings and, when it retreated, it left debris scattered everywhere and dangerous holes in the ground where the manhole covers used to be.

As workers scrambled in the dark to restart the power, a series of aftershocks then started to rock the plant. The loss of electricity meant there was no monitoring equipment, and the control room was offline. It also meant it was extremely difficult for the workers to keep the reactors cool.

By about 6:50 p.m., the reactor cores started suffering damage from the lack of coolant.

At 5:46 a.m. next morning, workers were finally able to start injecting fresh water into the cores to keep them cool but they didn't have enough on hand. At this point, the only way to have stopped a meltdown was to have pumped the only available coolant left – salt water – into the reactors. But since this would ruin the reactors permanently, officials delayed giving the OK until the evening, when it was too late.

The intense heat from the meltdowns destroyed the plant's containment infrastructure and radiation spewed out over several square miles of Japan. Once the nuclear fuel cladding contacted the water, it created dangerous hydrogen gas, which caused chemical explosions, creating more damage.

The Japanese government's emergency protocol called for the Nuclear and Industrial Safety Agency (NISA) to play the lead role in any nuclear plant accident. That meant even the Prime Minister's Office – called the Kantei – was supposed to take a back seat in such a case. If the Prime Minister wanted information, he was supposed to go through a regional nuclear response team for information and updates in such a case.

But the loss of power crippled communications around the country, including those for various organizations responsible for coordinating a response to a nuclear disaster.

The Secretariat of the Nuclear Emergency Response headquarters of NISA was supposed to gather information about the accident and the response to it, but couldn't. The Regional Nuclear Response Team was supposed to issue an evacuation order, but it was overwhelmed, as were the Crisis Management Center and the Nuclear Safety Commission.

All these groups were paralyzed. Each had important roles to play but all three were stuck without basic tools of communication.

On March 15th, four days after the accident, the Japanese Prime Minister, Naoto Kan, was scared and angry. The country was paralyzed by the triple disasters and very little was getting done effectively. Kan thought the emergency response was too slow and disorganized so he took charge. He ignored the protocol and started contacting the headquarters of the company that maintained the Fukushima plant, the Tokyo Electric Power Company (TEPCO), bypassing NISA.

The Kantei and TEPCO quickly created their own response team, even though this body had no legal authority. They assembled an ad hoc group that was politically well-connected but short on experts or anyone who had a ground-level understanding of the unfolding disaster – mainly politicians and advisors, along with the chairman of NISA.

Such was their inexperience that the PM himself did not know the country's emergency response to the Fukushima catastrophe could not officially begin until he issued a Declaration of a Nuclear Emergency Situation. It was a full two hours after he was advised about it that he issued it.

Not surprisingly, the Prime Minister's ad hoc response team cracked quickly under the pressure, as well as a lack of sleep and food. The Prime Minister himself decided to personally take charge.

Not knowing TEPCO and regulators had made a decision about venting and injection of seawater, Kan started issuing his own orders on the topic, making matters worse and slowing the work.

Kan also started ordering evacuations and setting up his own evacuation zones because he thought the group that had that responsibility – the Secretariat of the Nuclear Emergency Response Headquarters – was taking too long.

Kan continued making mistakes. Frustrated with a lack of communication from Fukushima, he left his office in Tokyo and visited the plant itself, but he only made things worse. Due to the presence of the Prime Minister, the emergency response slowed, causing disorder and confusion. Workers were surprised by his visit and had to balance the instructions they were receiving from him with ones they were getting from emergency officials.

The Prime Minister's intervention also caused a bureaucratic paralysis. Bureaucrats who were supposed to be issuing orders and making decisions suddenly became passive, eager to defer to the Prime Minister as a way of avoiding responsibility.

Other areas of government also began to break down in the hours and days afterwards.

The Fukushima Prefecture had an emergency response system, but in the scope of the disaster it found itself overwhelmed. It was set up to respond to either an earthquake/tsunami or a nuclear accident, but not both. In the confusion following the accident, and with normal communications impossible, the prefecture and the national government operated independently.

The Fukushima prefecture unilaterally ordered all residents living within two kilometres to evacuate the area. A half-hour later, the national government declared a three-kilometre evacuation area. Ironically, few were confused by the conflicting edicts since most forms of emergency communication systems were down and neither government could effectively reach the general public.

When communications were improved, the content of future messages from both levels of government was confusing. For example, while urging quick evacuations, a cabinet secretary repeatedly declared there was no immediate danger to the public. If there was no danger, people asked, then why do we have to leave?

This confusion at the higher levels had highly disruptive effects on the ground. The exclusion zone was expanded from three kilometres to 10, then 20, all in a single day. Evacuation destinations and other details were often revised.

Some residents assumed they would be away only a few days and packed lightly. Others were moved to areas with high radiation readings. Hospitals in the evacuation zones had enormous difficulty finding transportation for their patients and 60 patients died the first month from evacuation difficulties.

On March 15, those living between 20 km (12.4 miles) and 30 km (18.6 miles) were told to "shelter in place," meaning they should stay in their homes but keep their doors and windows closed and shut off any heating, ventilation and air conditioning. Unfortunately, it was several weeks before they received any new orders, and they had to survive a long time without basic necessities, or much news from the outside world. Eventually, they were told they could leave if they wanted to, but they received no explanation why the order had changed, so they were left even more confused and angry.

On March 23, some areas in the 30 km zone were found to have high radiation levels but it was a month later that they, too, were evacuated.

The chaos and disorganization following the nuclear disaster killed an unknown number of people, but many heartbreaking stories emerged in the days afterward. For example, the Guardian newspaper said:

• More than 125 elderly Japanese patients in a hospital near the nuclear plant were abandoned by medical staff, and at least 14 died.

• At least 11 Japanese seniors died in a retirement home without power, the paper said.

• And fourteen seniors died after being moved to a temporary shelter in a school gym from their hospital, which was in an evacuation zone.

The National Police Agency of Japan said in September, 2011, the tsunami and its effects killed a total of 15,861 people and injured 6,107, while a further 3,018 were still missing.

Ultimately, the amount of radiation that escaped into the atmosphere was deemed to have been only about one tenth of that at Chernobyl.

Indeed, no one died directly from radiation poisoning, though many of the workers who heroically stayed behind to restore power and contain the radiation were exposed to more radiation than is deemed to be healthy for an entire lifetime.

Many square miles of land around the plant were contaminated with radiation and many health officials are expecting cancer rates in the area to spike in the coming years.

Their country's poor response to the nuclear disaster enraged many Japanese, as they had been assured their country's nuclear power plants were perfectly safe.

Japanese emergency officials had long been prepared for a single disaster, and even had plans on how to handle two at the same time. But emergency officials had not contemplated having to deal with three simultaneously. This led to a cascading series of communications failures as the country's decision-makers struggled to cope with so many urgent situations all at once.

To find out why the country had been so ill-prepared, the Japanese parliament created the Fukushima Nuclear Accident Independent Investigation Commission, to be chaired by Kiyoshi Kurokawa, a medical doctor and former president of the Science Council of Japan.

Kurokawa's report was released on July 5, 2012. In it, he concluded that while the earthquake and tsunami were obviously natural disasters, the nuclear failure "was a profoundly manmade disaster that could and should have been foreseen and prevented. And its effects could have been mitigated by a more effective human response."

"The direct causes were all foreseeable prior to March 11, 2011," the report said. Despite public expectations, the Fukushima plant was "incapable of withstanding the earthquake and tsunami that hit" because

TEPCO and its regulatory bodies "all failed to develop the most basic safety requirements," it added.

The investigation found there was dangerous and negligent collusion among the plant managers and the agencies overseeing them to avoid making the necessary improvements and upgrades.

The commission also exposed many failures of communications, in particular by the Prime Minister and his office which, in the critical period just after the accident, did not promptly declare a state of emergency. Also, the Kantei contacted TEPCO and the Fukushima site directly, contrary to protocol, disrupting the chain of command. It also criticized the Prime Minister's visit to the plant to direct the workers dealing with the damaged cores as severely counter-productive.

"This unprecedented direct intervention by the Kantei diverted the attention and time of the on-site operational staff and confused the line of command."

There was such confusion that officials didn't realize they actually had some good ways to communicate. The report found the Secretariat of the Nuclear Emergency Response headquarters actually had a functioning teleconference system connected to the Prime Minister's Office and emergency organizations but there's no evidence it was used. TEPCO had a similar system but didn't connect it to the first one.

The report also found the evacuation was a mess and resulted in many needless deaths. The central government was not only slow in informing municipal governments about the nuclear power plant accident, but it also failed to convey the severity of the accident.

The commission found TEPCO responsible, too.

When the accident struck, neither the chairman or the president of TEPCO were immediately reachable, something the report calls "inconceivable."

It also said the plant's safety equipment to be used in severe accidents turned out to be less resistant to nuclear radiation than the normal equipment. In other words, when massive doses of radiation were spewing from the melting cores, employees were asked to don clothing that exposed them to more radiation not less.

Furthermore, during the initial stages of the accident, workers discovered sections in the diagrams of the severe accident instruction manual were missing. That means at the outset of the crisis, when time was critically short and tensions were high, the people tasked with stopping the meltdown had to flip through a flawed manual with a flashlight in the dark.

After the accident, TEPCO had two responsibilities – contain the accident and disclose facts about it in a timely way.

The report said TEPCO's disclosure of facts was "inappropriate, and that such inappropriateness was also an indirect cause of the deterioration of the situation." The report said TEPCO was selective about the information it chose to release – publicizing the injection of seawater into a reactor vessel but not mentioning an increase in radiation dosage that happened two-to-four hours earlier – and that it delayed releasing other information unnecessarily. In another instance, TEPCO said it withheld information about an increase in reactor pressure because it said the PMO forbade its release, when in fact, the PMO asked only that it be informed first.

The commission made several recommendations, including:

•   Create a permanent committee of the National Diet to oversee the regulators.

•   Reform the crisis management system to delineate the responsibilities of local and national governments, and the operators of nuclear power plants.

•   Establish a clear chain of command for emergencies.

- Reform the corporate structure of TEPCO.

- Establish a new nuclear regulatory agency.

A total of 146,520 residents were evacuated by government due to the nuclear accident, though more left on their own accord.

About a year later, a survey by mail of 21,000 evacuees in 12 cities, towns and villages was done. A total of 10,633 people responded.

The results showed a surprising delay in the dissemination of information. Only about one in 10 people knew about the nuclear accident the evening it happened, despite releases of information at 3:42 p.m. and 4:45 p.m. and a declaration of a state of emergency at 7:03 p.m.

Only 20 per cent of the residents of the town where the plant was located knew about the accident when evacuation from the three-kilometre zone was ordered at 9:23 p.m. March 11th.

It was only when people got up the next morning that awareness in the entire evacuation area rose past 50 per cent, and not until dinner time the next day when it hit about 90 per cent.

In analyzing the survey, the results showed municipalities were highly successful in communicating the information to their residents. However, the municipalities often relied on getting that information from the federal government which often failed to pass it on, leaving critical instructions unbroadcast.

When people finally got the evacuation order, they did not get enough information about the situation to be useful for their evacuation. Some people left in such a hurry they fled without necessary medicine or enough clothing. Others thought they would only be a way for a day or two and only took the bare necessities, but realized their mistake only when they were on the jammed highways out of town. Some thought the emergency was related to another tsunami, and not a nuclear accident.

The confusion and fear of the residents is evident in the written comments they made to the pollsters, some of which are included below:

A resident of Futaba:

"I left my house with only the bare necessities. I learned where to go through the emergency radio system while I was on the road. I arrived at the first evacuation site where I was instructed to go, taking 6 hours by car instead of only 1 hour in an ordinary situation. On my way there, my son who lives away called and told me that I should not expect to return soon. Only then did I start to recognize little by little what was actually happening."

A resident of Okuma:

"If there had been even a word about a nuclear power plant when the evacuation was ordered, we could have reacted reasonably, taken our valuables with us or locked up the house before we had left. We had to run with nothing but the clothes we were wearing.

A resident of Tomioka:

"We wanted to hear clearly that we would not be able to return for a while. I couldn't bring my valuables with me. In particular, because records of medical treatment were left at home, my parents' conditions worsened during evacuation. It is hard especially for elderly people to flee unprepared."

A resident of Namie:

"I managed to spend a night in an elementary school in Tsushima district after hearing an announcement in the town gymnasium in the morning of March 12 that a tsunami had approached Namie-Higashi Junior High School, instead of being told of the accident at the nuclear power plant. If I had been told specifically about the accident, I would have evacuated to somewhere further than Tsushima. It is disappointing that information was not given."

A resident of the Odaka ward of Minamisoma:

"We didn't know there was a hydrogen explosion at the plant, so we couldn't guess why we had to evacuate. The director (of TEPCO) at the time of the accident recalled on TV that he thought he might die at the time, but that sort of information should have been announced to the nearby residents instantly. In any event, information was released too slowly. The residents have not been treated properly."

A resident of Kawauchi:

"On March 11, immediately after hearing first news of the accident, many people in the village evacuated to this area. Young people were emailing 'evacuate' to each other, almost like chain mail. However, we did not receive any official information on the evacuation. We were only told to stay indoors through the emergency radio system. After hearing a neighbor who has a policeman in his family say, 'I'm going to evacuate because it seems dangerous,' I decided to evacuate. I heard that the police had left Kawauchi by March 14. The volunteers who were giving out food had used up the remaining gasoline for their transportation. I wanted them to help us evacuate as early as possible. I can only think that they abandoned us."

A resident of Kawamata:

"They went on to say that there is no immediate effect, but the evacuation was explained on April 16. If they explained earlier, I could have found a specific place to evacuate. Although it was a large disaster, the response was too slow. The most important initial response based on the facts of the actual situation was not present and no orders based on 'measures in conformity' were given."

Some of the angriest comments were understandably from the people who were moved to areas initially considered safe, but then later declared evacuation zones. About 70 percent of the residents of Futaba, Okuma, Tomioka, Naraha and Namie had to evacuate four times or more.

A resident of Namie:

"The fact that I evacuated to an area with the highest radiation dose in the absence of (radiation monitoring data) remains a source of fear for my health for the rest of my life. Why didn't they disclose the information."

A resident of Minamisoma:

"I wish the information had been disclosed much earlier. I understand that the decision by the government not to disclose was intended to prevent a possible panic. But residents were evacuated to areas with high concentrations of radiation because of the lack of information.

A Resident of Namie:

"On the afternoon of March 11, when we were just about to patch the roof we were told to evacuate to the gym of the nearby Tsushima school. We stayed in the school for 3 or 4 days. It was a place with high radiation levels. We moved six places inside and outside of the prefecture and finally stopped after coming here."

A resident of Tomioka:

"We had no clue what was going on but we were told to evacuate to Kawauchi. When we got there, we had to move from place to place and finally arrived at Miharu but we were told that it was full. We were told to go to the evacuation center in Motomiya. We later moved several times after that and are currently staying in a rental in Iwaki. Since then one year has passed but we have no idea of what we are going to do."

133

A similar survey was done of workers at the Fukushima plant and it showed confusion there, too. It said there were too few devices to measure radiation in the plant, there were no reports on the cumulative radiation dose of individual workers, and no efforts were made to manage internal radiation. It found many workers were frustrated and anxious over the lack of worker radiation dose checks. Some had to share one dosimeter with several others, and a few had no dosimeters at all. About 30 per cent of workers were not told their cumulative dosage.

Only about 40 per cent of TEPCO workers were warned the reactors were or could be in a dangerous state. Only about 10 per cent of subcontractor workers involved in dealing with the accident received an explanation in advance about the possibility the plant having a nuclear accident.

Of those on the site, 30 per cent of TEPCO employees and 40 per cent of subcontracted workers had not agreed to deal with such an accident.

A TEPCO employee:

"There was no explanation at all about how dangerous it was until the early morning of March 15. I understand that it was a difficult situation and there was limited time to give explanations, but at least we wanted to be informed."

Another TEPCO employee:

"We were supposed to manage our cumulative radiation exposure level on our own, perhaps because the database became unavailable due to the earthquake. But we didn't even have pen or paper. We had no way to accurately keep track."

Another TEPCO employee:

"Workers in the main anti-earthquake building were laboring under conditions where they couldn't trust anyone but themselves, and they were the only ones responsible for their own safety. Don't all of these problems stem from a fundamental lack of preparedness for disaster? I don't want to hear that this event occurred because it was 'unanticipated.' The government and the power company are accountable for the preexisting problems that led to the disaster."

A subcontractor employee:

"No information whatsoever about the station blackout was delivered to the end-workers like us. I had to learn about the emergency evacuation orders for residents within 20km of the plant from TV.... I finally managed to call our Tokyo head office on March 14, but they were not aware that there were still employees working in the main anti-earthquake building. I asked to evacuate, but they declined my request.'"

A primary contractor employee:

"For workers, there were almost no evacuation instructions. There has to be a clearly understood protocol for communicating information. Measures taken in response to the accident were uncoordinated and poor overall. This is also true from the perspective of the residents. Evacuation procedures and destinations were vague and still remain so."

Comment by a subordinate contractor employee

"On the news it was reported that the plant workers who were dealing with the accident were prepared to die, but I was watching the news, thinking that there is no way we were ready to die."

It is clear there was a catastrophic failure to communicate properly at many, many levels, from the prime minister who disregarded the chain of command to the emergency officials constantly shifting the evacuation area.

While it would have been too much to expect everyone in the area to get a full rundown of the details of the accident, far too many were not even told there had been an accident at all.

And while the government did have a legitimate concern about creating a panic, it erred far too much on the side of not giving even basic details.

Simply put, the people around the nuclear plant should have been told the following details as soon as possible:

1.　　The Fukushima nuclear plant has been crippled by the tsunami and is leaking radiation.

2.　　We don't know how much radiation is leaking yet but we feel it's important that everyone within 50 kilometers of the plant leave the area within 72 hours.

3.　　We don't know how long you will need to be away, so please take personal belongings to last you for a week. This includes medicine and cold-weather clothing.

4.　　If you have relatives outside the 50-kilometer zone, please ask to stay with them until further notice. Otherwise, please contact government officials to find the best destination.

Would some people have panicked? Probably, yes. But far more would have made better choices about what to take and where to go.

The lesson here is that during an emergency, it's best to tell the public what you know is true and not try to put a filter on it. Also, make sure to anticipate the question "why" in your communications. Don't assume people know any details. There's no problem in repeating old information (unless it is out of date) but there is a problem when people don't know what you're talking about.

In journalism, reporters are taught to ask the five "W"s – who, what, where, when, why. It's a good rule for officials in an emergency, too. When people are told to evacuate an area, they're going to have many questions. Try to answer the most common ones. In this disaster, it appears the federal government didn't want to appear un-authoritative or uncertain about what it knew. It also appears that its messages weren't clear enough for most people to make decisions.

Another important point is to repeat important information. You never know when someone you need to reach is listening or distracted. Don't expect your audience to be watching TV, listening to the radio or on the internet at the time your message goes out. And some people aren't sure they heard the message right the first time anyway, so repetition can help reduce rumors and exaggeration.

Also, use every kind of media at your disposal. If the power is out, why not ask a printer in another part of the country to run off a few thousand copies of the evacuation order and truck them to the evacuation areas where they could be handed out? You could then follow that up with copies of answers to a list of common questions, including phone numbers to call and websites to visit when the power does come back. In fact, the governments in Japan could have set up an impromptu free daily newspaper, distributed by volunteers, so that people in areas without power could have had a better idea of what was going on.

Ultimately, it appears the most lethal part of the 2011 nuclear disaster in Japan was not radiation but lack of information.

10

Air France Flight 447

It was about 2 a.m. on June 1st, 2009 and Air France flight 447 was halfway across the Atlantic on a flight to Paris from Rio de Janeiro, cruising at 35,000 feet. On board were 12 crew and 216 passengers. The Airbus 330 had just entered a massive, but common, storm found around the equator called an inter-tropical convergence but the flight was relatively smooth, everything was functioning normally and the passengers were asleep.

At 2:02 a.m., co-pilot David Robert re-entered the cockpit after taking a rest and Capt. Marc Dubois decided the time was right for him to take a nap, too, so he gave up his left-side seat to Robert and went in the back to close his eyes. Since the flight was quite uneventful, he decided to leave the controls in the care of the man in the right-hand chair, the other co-pilot, Pierre-Cedric Bonin, despite the fact Bonin had considerably less experience than Robert.

As he was getting comfortable in his seat, Robert noticed the plane's radar hadn't been calibrated properly so he adjusted it. Once it corrected, he noticed the plane was actually heading straight towards an area of severe turbulence.

At 2:08 a.m., Robert suggested Bonin veer left to get around it and Bonin made the course adjustment but it was too late to avoid heading straight into a massive thunderhead.

At 2:10 a.m. the cockpit was suddenly filled with a roar as the jet was buffeted by storm-force winds. Suddenly, the devices that determined the plane's speed, the pitot tubes, iced over and the plane's computer started receiving wildly differing and fluctuating speeds. The calculated airspeed reading dropped suddenly from 274 knots to 156 knots. A backup system displayed the speed going from 275 to 139 knots before going back to 223. Meanwhile, another indicator, showed a drop from Mach 0.80 (eight tenths of the speed of sound) to 0.26.

The incoherent data forced the autopilot to disconnect and hand full control back to the pilots.

Bonin, the junior co-pilot, assured his more senior colleague that he had the controls – "J'ai les commandes" – and then he pulled back on his stick to take the jet into a steep climb to go over the storm.

Bonin did this despite having agreed with his colleague just a few minutes before that the Airbus couldn't climb further because the atmosphere was too thin and the jet was still too heavy with fuel.

The plane's computer then sounded a chime to alert the pilots they were leaving their assigned altitude, and this was followed by a stall warning.

A jet's stall warning is designed to be clear, unambiguous and impossible to ignore. It is common among all kinds of aircraft – a computer voice shouts "stall, stall!" followed by an intentionally irritating sound similar to that of a cricket.

onse to a stall is also supposed to be clear. From the

hool, pilots are taught to push the stick forward to put

, so that it can regain airspeed and control.

in nor Robert talked about the stall. Rather they

of the airspeed indicator.

got a good, we haven't got a good display."

the, the, the speeds so … engine thrust A T H R (auto-

hrust."

to climb at a rate of about 7,000 feet per minute,

d to just 93 knots, or about 105 miles per hour.

peed. Watch your speed.

ing back down.

. According to the (altimeter) you're going up so go

ack down.

going down.

At 2:10:34, the left-hand pitot tube unfroze and began reading a valid speed of 223 knots, a drop of (?) knots since the autopilot disconnected. This is because the plane had suddenly risen to around 37,000 feet, having climbed about 2,000 feet in 30 seconds, far too steep to maintain airspeed.

Robert: "You're at, go back down."

Bonin: "It's going, we're going back down."

Robert: "Descend!"

Bonin: "Here we go, we're descending."

Robert: "Softly!"

Bonin had not in fact started descending, he was merely slowing the plane's rate of climb, but the co-pilots believed the plane had leveled off. The stall warning stopped as the plane's speed increased to 223 knots and the co-pilots breathed sighs of relief. But Bonin was still rattled by what happened so he called the pilot back to the cockpit.

At 2:10:51, however, Bonin again pulled back on the stick and the stall alarm restarted. Bonin cursed.

Despite the bad weather outside, the pitot tubes started working again, so both co-pilots had the correct speed readings to fly the plane. And yet, Bonin kept his stick pulled back trying to climb up and over the storm. The problem with this plan was the same as before – the plane was too heavy and the altitude was too high – and it is completely unnecessary. If Bonin had just flown level, the stall alarm would have stopped.

In the 30 seconds since the first stall warning, the airplane's speed dropped from 205 knots to about 160. At 2:11:10, the altitude hit its maximum of 38,000 feet, before the plane started to descend.

Robert: "But we've got the engines...what's happening?

Robert cursed because the Captain had still not responded to their request to return to the cockpit.

Robert: "Damn it, is he coming or not? We've got the engines. What's happening?"

Bonin: "Damn it, I don't have control of the plane any more now. I don't have control of the plane at all!"

Robert, the more senior co-pilot, then said he's taking control of the plane but he doesn't do any better. He, too, pulled back on the stick, and the stall warning continued to sound. After a moment, Bonin took control back.

At this point, the plane had long stopped climbing and was now plummeting towards the ocean at a rate of 6,800 feet per minute and the forward speed has dropped from Mach 0.51 to 0.42. Because Bonin was consistently pulling back on his stick, the plane's nose was up 30 degrees. All these facts were displayed on the plane's instruments.

At 2:11:42, the plane was at 36,000 feet, moving forward at about 108 knots and descending at 9,100 feet per minute. The nose was angled upward at 12 degrees and both engines were at full acceleration.

The stall warning continued to sound as the captain returns to the cockpit.

Dubois: "What the hell are you doing?"

Bonin: "We've lost control of the plane!"

Robert: "We've totally lost control of the plane. We don't understand at all. We've tried everything."

The stall warning stops and then restarted. The plane was nose up at more than 40 degrees and falling fast, but the cockpit crew were baffled.

Bonin: "I have a problem it's that I don't have vertical speed indication."

Dubois: "OK."

Bonin: "I have no more displays. I have the impression that we have some crazy speed, no? What do you think?"

The stall warning continued to sound and co-pilot Robert implored the captain for advice, but none was forthcoming. They were at 30,000 feet and falling fast.

Robert: "What do you think about it? What do you think? What do we need to do?"

Dubois: "There. I don't know. There, it's going down."

Bonin: "That's good. We should be wings level. No, it won't..."

Dubois: "The wings to flat horizon, the standby horizon."

Robert: "The horizon. The speed?" The stall warning sounds again. "You're climbing! You're going down, down, down, down."

Bonin: "Am I going down now?"

Robert: "Go down."

Dubois: "No, you climb here."

Bonin: "I'm climbing, OK, so we're going down."

At this point, at 2:12:44 a.m., the plane is at 20,000 feet and almost in a free fall, with its nose up. The captain is baffled.

Dubois: "It's impossible."

Bonin: "On altitude, what do we have?

Robert: "What do you mean on altitude?"

Bonin: "Yeah, yeah, yeah I'm going down, no?"

Robert: "You're going down, yes."

Dubois: "Hey, you're in...get the wings horizontal. Get the wings horizontal."

Bonin: "That's what I'm trying to do."

Dubois: "Get the wings horizontal."

The stall warning continued to sound. Bonin still had his stick pulled back.

At 2:13:32 the plane was at 10, 092 feet. That meant it had fallen about 10,000 feet in 48 seconds. Four seconds later, it was at 9,332 feet.

Bonin: "Nine thousand feet."

Robert: "Climb, climb, climb, climb!"

Bonin: "But I've been at maxi nose-up for a while."

Dubois: "No, no, no! Don't climb!"

Robert: "So go down. So give me the controls, the controls to me."

Bonin gave control to Robert, who – at long last – pushed the nose of the plane down to gather speed. But it was too late. The plane was at 4,000 feet and just seconds away from impact.

Dubois: "Watch out, you're pitching up there!"

Robert: "I'm pitching up?

Bonin: "Well we need to. We are at four thousand feet."

Computer voice: "Pull up! Pull up! Pull up!"

Dubois: "Go on, pull!"

Bonin: "Let's go! Pull up! Pull up! Pull up!"

Computer voice: "Pull up! Pull up! Pull up! Pull up!"

Robert: "Damn it, we're going to crash! This can't be happening!"

Bonin: "But what's happening?"

Captain: "Ten degrees of pitch."

The plane slams into the ocean. There are no survivors.

Analysis:

The jet fell into an especially deep and remote part of the Atlantic Ocean and it took nearly two years for searchers to find the black boxes.

Once analyzed, the flight data and voice recordings showed the cockpit crew apparently oblivious to the fact their plane was falling out of the sky, and that their actions were the cause.

The French BEA (Bureau d'Enquetes et d'Analyses pour la securite d l'aviation civile) had already issued two interim reports on the crash by the time the black boxes were found, so it issued a third, which it published July 29, 2011. With the extra knowledge, it was able to make several conclusions, including:

• There was an inconsistency in speed readings, following the blockage of the pitot tubes.

• The faulty speed readings on the left Primary Flight Display lasted 29 seconds and the speed reading on the Integrated Standby Instrument System was invalid for 54 seconds.

• Neither of the pilots made any reference to the stall warning.

• Neither of the pilots formally identified the stall situation.

• The stall warning was triggered continuously for 54 seconds.

• The engines functioned normally and always responded to the crew's inputs.

• No announcement was made to the passengers.

The question on everyone's mind was why the pilots never properly reacted to the stall warnings until too late.

The BEA report makes some educated guesses:

It appears Bonin's decision to pull back on his stick made matters worse, not just by stalling the aircraft but by confusing the on-board computer so much it stopped issuing stall warnings. That's because then the aircraft slowed to below 60 knots, its computer ceased calculating the angle of attack and stopped feeding certain information to the pilots, as it was programmed to do.

This meant that every time Bonin did the right thing by pushing his stick forward to reduce his climb, the airplane sped up and the sensors reactivated, triggering the stall warnings. Bonin would then pull up once more, the plane would slow down and the stall warnings would cease. This happened over and over. The pilots were jolted by stall warnings every time they did the right thing.

The BEA also noted when the Captain left the cockpit to go for a short nap, he did not leave his two co-pilots with "any clear operational instructions, in particular on the role of each of the two copilots." The lack of any formal sharing of duties among equals might have led to their confusion, it said.

The co-pilots also failed to follow protocol by calling out to each other their readings of the highly unusual speed, pitch and altitude, to ensure the other was made aware of them.

Not leaving the copilots with instructions and not calling out unusual readings, are both violations of the concept of Crew Resource Management (see chapter one) where roles are clearly defined and pilots share critical information.

Another potential problem was first raised in an article by the magazine Popular Mechanics. In a Boeing cockpit, all controls are linked, so if one pilot moves his stick forward, the other pilot's will move forward, too, and the stick will stay in that position until the pilot moves it again.

This is not the case in an Airbus, where controls are operated independently. Once a pilot lets go of his control stick, it returns to a neutral position, just like the joystick for a home computer. Airbus considers this an improvement over Boeing's design because the company says pilots have to adjust their controls less often.

But critics say it means pilots cannot tell where a switch or lever is set by looking at it or touching it. Instead, they have to check their computer screens.

This design may have played a role in the Air France crash because, the theory goes, if the copilots had been in a Boeing, Robert would have known right away Bonin had his stick pulled back for almost the entire emergency, because his stick would have been back, too. Sadly, in this case, the left hand didn't know what the right hand was doing.

The key communication failure here was Robert and Dubois not knowing Bonin had his stick pulled all the way back. As soon as Bonin said what he was doing out loud -- "But I've been at maxi nose-up for a while" – Dubois knew right away what was wrong. He took control of the plane to bring it out of its stall, but it was too late. They were doomed.

In retrospect, Bonin's actions should have been obvious to the other two pilots, and indeed the jet was trying to tell them what he was doing, too. The altimeter showed they were plummeting and the computer voice was shouting "Stall!" at them for several minutes.

But all this confusion could have been lifted if Captain Dubois, upon entering the cockpit, had just asked Bonin to say – out loud – what actions he was taking. Bonin would have said "I'm at maxi-nose up," and Dubois would have told him to dive, to pick up speed. Problem solved.

Even though they were surrounded by modern technology, the pilots just needed to do a better job of talking to each other, as prescribed in the Cockpit Resource Management system, and everyone on board would have arrived safely in France a few hours later.

11

Code Red

So now that we've seen how not to communicate, what should we do with this knowledge? In an average day for the average person, very little, because most conversations you will have aren't terribly important. But what happens when you're having a conversation that is important? What if you really need to make sure the person you're talking to understands you?

Firstly, when making plans, you can ask them to repeat back to you what you just said, to confirm they understood correctly. For example, if you want to meet a lawyer for lunch, but you know he will start billing you from the time he sits down at the restaurant whether you're there or not, you should ask him to confirm the meeting place after you say it. It might take some social skills to find the right way to do this without sounding strange.

Client: "Just so I know we're talking about the same place, you know where we're going, right?"

Lawyer: "Sure. O'Hanrahan's."

Client: "Which one were you thinking of?"

Lawyer: "The one on 39th Street. Does that work for you?"

Client: "Yep. The one on 39th Street. Across from the Sears, right?"

Lawyer: "Yes. That's the one."

Client: "I have the address as 1414 39th Street. Does that sound right?"

Lawyer: "Sounds right."

This kind of clarification can easily expose most latent misunderstandings. Depending on the importance of the meeting, a person might also want to say out loud the date, day of the week and the time of day just to be sure. It might even be a good idea to exchange emails to confirm the details, or even email a meeting request. That way there can be several layers of confirmation.

Client: "OK. I'll see you tomorrow, the 15th."

Lawyer: "Tomorrow? I thought we were talking about Wednesday."

Client: "Tomorrow is Wednesday, right?"

Lawyer: "Is it? Let me check."

Client: "Ooops, I'm wrong. Sorry. You're right. Wednesday is the 15th."

Lawyer: "Wednesday, the 15th."

Client: "Just to go over it again – noon, on Wednesday, December 15th, lunch at O'Hanrahan's at 1414 39th Street.

Lawyer: "Correct."

By speaking out loud, you can make sure you're both "on the same page." If you sit quietly and assume you were understood, you're taking a risk. If the risk is buying your date the wrong flavor of ice cream, the worst result might be that you're single next Saturday night.

Boy: "I thought you said bacon flavor."

Girl: "I said pecan."

The main problem with asking for clarification and repetition is it can run contrary to our social conventions. You can't go around verifying every bit of information you get or you'll irritate everyone. On matters of little importance, you will have to make silent assumptions about what you hear or read, and you'll have to accept the occasional misunderstanding. Because language is a kind of code, you can designate these conversations as Code Green, meaning you can proceed as normal. Go right through the conversation without looking.

For more important conversations, perhaps like the one above, you can designate them Code Yellow, meaning you should be cautious about making assumptions before proceeding with your plans.

But when it comes to matters of great importance, such as when human lives are at stake, you'll want to avoid making any assumptions at all. This would be considered Code Red. Stop what you're doing and triple-confirm every detail. Get everyone involved to repeat back to you their understanding of the situation and their responsibilities. Include redundancies in the conversation, like emailing everyone the instructions you just told them in person and getting them to confirm they understand by replying. Rehearsals are a good idea. Plan for glitches. And so on.

Airline pilots operate on Code Red all the time, even during a routine flight, only they call it Cockpit Resource Management (see Chapter 1). All critical information is checked and rechecked. The pilots are supposed to talk to each other when making decisions. If the co-pilot disagrees with something the captain does, he can speak up as long as he's respectful.

So, the moral of this book is: The next time you find yourself in an important conversation, take a moment and imagine you're an airline pilot. Didn't you always want to be a pilot?

Made in the USA
Charleston, SC
02 December 2013